PRAISE FOR
Inconceivable Redemption

Inconceivable Redemption is a superb companion for women who have experienced pregnancy loss. After my losses I felt so alone and grappled with many spiritual questions. I would have loved to have had this book to help me along that journey. Erin provides much-needed hope for mourners and helps women point their weary hearts to Jesus. This book will bless countless readers in the same way that it has blessed me.

～ Sarah Philpott, PhD author of the award-winning book, Loved Baby: 31 Devotions Helping You Grieve and Cherish Your Child After Pregnancy Loss. Connect with Sarah at allamericanmom.net.

Erin's journey gives permission and freedom to allow our momma hearts to fully embrace both the rawness of loss and the hope we can have in the God who heals and redeems the most broken pieces. Having struggled with infertility and the loss of my own twin boys born prematurely, I resonated with her beautifully journaled thoughts and feelings. As a pastor, I will recommend this book as a go-to resource to help other women who have traveled this painfully unexpected road to redemption.

～ Tanya Whitaker, Small Groups Pastor, River Pointe Church

Erin Greneaux understands all too well the heartbreak of miscarriage. In *Inconceivable Redemption*, she poignantly describes the devastating loss of her first child as one of the most difficult and loneliest seasons of her life. Those who were closest to her were sympathetic, but they couldn't fully understand the painful emotions she was going through. Words of consolation from others and announcements of friends' pregnancies and birth announcements caused pain, resentment and confusion.

Feeling as though she was the only person in the world without a baby, she was surprised to find that there were countless other women experiencing the same kind of trauma, only no one was talking about it. Hearing similar stories of tragedy helped her realize that, although each person's experience was unique, every loss is significant.

Like others in her situation, she had to painfully walk through the stages of shock, denial, mood swings, jealousy, anger, forgetfulness and questioning God before she found light at the end of the dark tunnel of grief.

Meaningful scriptures and honest personal diary entries offer enlightening truth, hope and encouragement to anyone who has experienced the tragedy of miscarriage. Readers will find comfort and emotional healing as their pain is acknowledged and they are given permission to embrace it.

   Bev DeSalvo, Pastor's wife, speaker and author of Return to Joy: Finding Healing in the Arms of Your Savior

I wish there had been a book like this 25 years ago as I began my long infertility journey. Erin writes with much sincerity, compassion, and candor as she takes you through her own wandering through infertility and miscarriage and seeing the hand of God through it all. Prepare to hear from the Lord for yourself as you walk with her through these pages.
 — Susan Reeves, 35 yr. staff member with Campus Crusade, mother of two adopted daughters and grandmother of two grandchildren

Erin's courageous story of muddling through her crisis of faith through miscarriage and waiting and trusting God is so inspiring. Her honesty about her grief, questions, heartache and journey of becoming God's child gives me hope to press on in surrendering my life and plans to Him. This is a must read for anyone who has experienced loss in pregnancy and also for those who want to know how to comfort and understand the depth of devastation and grief many women experience. Her story will give you hope and courage to believe God's goodness no matter how the story is written!
 — Barbara Culwell, Discipler of Women, CoreClarity Facilitator

Erin tenderly shares her heart in a sincere and vulnerable way that is sensitive to those who are currently hurting. As a single who has grieved (and often still does occasionally grieve) never marrying and not having children of my own, I was still very touched and found comfort in her words. The truths about God and His care for us that she reached while grieving miscarriage, are true for me, and true for you, too, no matter our personal areas of loss!

    ~ Kat McMullen, former morning show co-host at Peace 107.7 FM

    This book touched me, not only as a psychologist, but also as a mother who has experienced miscarriage. Erin's brilliant ability to portray her raw emotion associated with having a miscarriage provided comfort for me. Going through any experience associated with grief and loss can feel isolating. Erin's sharing of her private and unaltered thoughts made this experience more relatable. Her process of wrestling with her faith and being able to ultimately find comfort in God's promises to us was a great reminder of how we can all use His words to guide us and find our way through loss of hopes, dreams, and loved ones.

    ~ Donna Aucoin, PhD, MP and Assoc. Psychology Practice

    From beginning to end, I felt as if I were sitting and reliving so much of my own journey of infertility. Erin writes with such vulnerability and is able to take you to the depth of her pain while ultimately pointing the reader back to the One and only Hope, Jesus Christ. I wish that I had this book to read when I was going through infertility because Erin understands, and when one walks through infertility it can feel like no one understands and that you are all alone.

This book will no doubt become like a friend and a comforter to anyone who is struggling with infertility and/or miscarriage. It is often so easy to sit in self-pity and isolate ourselves from others when we go through such pain, but this book will serve as a way to connect women who are feeling stuck and need emotional, practical, and spiritual support during what can often seem like the loneliest time for women.

The biggest treasure found in this book is Jesus. Erin sensitively shares her heart but graciously and lovingly points the reader to Truth and reminds us all of the importance of being grounded in God's Truth as those are the only promises given to us. I cannot wait to share this book with the number of women I am connected to who are struggling with infertility. Erin is able to speak into that with much understanding and sensitivity knowing that every person's story is unique and has different endings. What isn't different are God's promises and His presence no matter our struggle! This book will help you take your eyes off your problems and put them back on God's promises.

Carita Chen, Global Mission Area Director for Cru City, 10-year infertility survivor, mother to an adopted son, see her viral adoption story video at https://www.youtube.com/watch?v=ZLOgtobOWHQ

Inconceivable
REDEMPTION

God's Presence in
Miscarriage & Infertility

———— ✺ ————

Erin Greneaux

Copyright 2019 Erin Greneaux

All rights reserved. No part of this publication may be reproduced, distributed, or transmitted in any form or by any means, including photocopying, recording, or other electronic or mechanical methods without the prior written permission of the publisher, except in the case of brief quotations embodied in critical reviews and certain other non-commercial uses permitted by copyright law. First printing 2019.

ISBN: Erin Greneaux
ISBN-13: 978-1-7336198-1-3

All scriptures marked NIV are from the Holy Bible, New International Version, NIV, Copyright 1973, 1978, 1984, 2011 by Biblica, Inc.

All scriptures marked MSG are taken from The Message. Copyrights 1993, 1994, 1995, 1996, 2000, 2001, 2002. Used by permission of NavPress Publishing Group.

All scriptures marked NLT are taken from The Holy Bible, New Living Translation, copyright 1996, 2004, 2015 by Tyndale House Foundation. Used by permission of Tyndale House Publishers, Inc., Carol Stream, Illinois 60188. All rights reserved.

ACKNOWLEDGEMENTS

    A heartfelt thank you to my husband, Nathan, for loving and supporting me during my journey through grief. I am so blessed to have you by my side in every season that we walk through together. The trials we face make the good moments that much sweeter!

    Thank you to Malary, Megan, Mattie, Wendy, and Rachael—the group of women who courageously worked through the memories of difficult seasons of pain and grief in order to evaluate the message portrayed in these pages. Your boldness, vulnerability, and sincerity enabled these words to better serve so many women as they walk the same process of grief that each of you share.

    Thank you Emily, for your amazing editing skills and Adriane, for your incredible cover design. Also, a heartfelt thank you to the many people who read the manuscript beforehand to offer reviews, suggestions, feedback, and promotion. This book has been such a group effort, and I am humbled by the many people who put their time and energy into making its message as relevant and healing as possible.

    Most importantly, I want to thank God for being who He says He is—good, faithful, sovereign, just, loving, gracious, merciful, Keeper of Promises, and my Redeemer! I can only share these words because of who He is and who He has redeemed me to be.

Contents

Acknowledgements	ix
Prologue	1
Excitement	6
Shock	18
Apprehension	32
Emotional Instability	42
Honesty	68
Impatience	90
Submission	108
Fear	124
Redemption	142
Epilogue	165
A Letter From God	169
About The Author	173
Pictures	175

*"Listen carefully:
Unless a grain of wheat is buried in the ground,
dead to the world,
it is never any more than a grain of wheat.
But if it is buried,
it sprouts and reproduces itself many times over.
In the same way,
anyone who holds on to life just as it is destroys that life.
But if you let it go, reckless in your love,
you'll have it forever, real and eternal."*

— John 12:24-25 (MSG)

PROLOGUE

Let me begin by telling you who I am not. I am not a professional. I am not a licensed counselor or a reproductive specialist, and I do not have a degree in theology. I am simply a woman who has walked the road that you are walking.

My story is not the worst one. It is not shocking. It would not make a great screenplay. Far from it! In fact, what I experienced is incredibly common. According to the American Pregnancy Association, fifty to seventy-five percent of pregnancies end in miscarriage, many of which occur before the mother even knows that she is carrying a baby[1].

I am sharing my story because it is so common; because I want you to know that you are not alone. I want you to be assured that the feelings, questions, and struggles that you are experiencing are completely normal. But more importantly, I want you to be encouraged that they are temporary, and that there is redemption on the other side. The grief process is very personal, and you will have to find your own answers as you work through it. The path is unclear and unique to each. However, I hope that my journey can offer a light with which to navigate.

It may seem like this book is about me losing a child, but it's really not. It's about the process of

---

[1] "Miscarriage." American Pregnancy Association. americanpregnancy.org/pregnancy-complications/miscarriage/.

me becoming a child: God's child. And I don't mean becoming a Christian, either. I gave my life to Christ as a child at the age of six and have walked with Him faithfully my whole life. But the process of becoming a child of God, of truly being redeemed, not only in His eyes, but also in mine, did not really develop until I walked through a loss that tested my faith. I invite you to walk with me through that journey of discovery, in hope that you will be able to find redemption in your story as well.

    If you have picked up this book, then it is likely that your story is filled with pain, loss, and grief. You may be wondering if the pieces of your life will ever be made whole again. You are probably trying to figure out what to do now. Let me encourage you, dear friend, there is hope! There is redemption. There is an abundant life in Christ, just as He promises. But it is a journey. God is writing a story, and sometimes we don't see the pieces come together until the last chapter. And those kinds of stories are often the best.

    I promise to be completely honest with you in these pages. I am not going to sugarcoat things. I'm not going to present my best self. I am taking down the smiling, social media picture and showing you the vulnerable, unedited version, because that is the one that God sees and loves. That is the one that He has redeemed.

    I am going to be including my personal journal entries in this book—entries that were never meant to see the light of day, that were written in moments of raw emotion. I am not going to edit them in any way. I am not going to skip entries, change wording, or take anything out. If I wrote it down during that time period, it is included. I'm not trying to change my story. I am also going to be adding in thoughts and actions that took place that I didn't write down at the time, because I was too ashamed or hurt to even put them into words. This is reality in its rawest form.

The only way that we can truly appreciate God's redemption is to learn to see ourselves the way that He does—full of flaws, but capable of being made whole and beautiful at the same time, because we are His children. I now invite you to enter into the most challenging season of my life.

ONE

EXCITEMENT

"A new baby is like the beginning of all things—wonder, hope, a dream of possibilities."

— *Eda J LeShan*

April 4, 2014

    Oh my gosh! I can't believe it! It's all I can say because it's really true for real—I'm PREGNANT! Nathan and I have planned for probably the last year and a half to finish paying off the house and then begin trying to have a baby at the beginning of this year. We paid off the house in January, started trying in February, and were successful in March!

    I'm so excited. I still can't believe it's true! I can't stop saying thank you, God, for this blessing, this amazing miracle! I took the test when I woke up this morning. I am a week late but still wasn't convinced because last month I was two and a half weeks late, and no baby. But when the test said "pregnant," I just started jumping up and down!

    Nathan was still asleep, so I took a shower, laughing with joy, so overwhelmed with happiness. He was still asleep, so I got dressed and ate breakfast. He woke up but was still groggy, so I tried hard not to blurt out the news until after he had taken his shower. I was hanging up clothes when he got out, and I couldn't keep from smiling.

    "What?" he asked.

    "Nothing," I told him, but I couldn't wipe the grin from my face.

    "No, what is it?" he asked again.

    I gave him a hug and said in his ear, "I'm pregnant."

    "No way! Oh my gosh, that's crazy!" he said, but he

EXCITEMENT

was smiling from ear to ear, "That's amazing!"

It was a perfect moment—we are going to be parents! Thank you, thank you, thank you, God, for this amazing miracle!

I have always wanted to be a mom. I was the child who had the Barbie minivan and all of the Barbie kids. My mom was a stay-at-home mom, and I couldn't think of anything that I would like to do more than to have a bunch of children. I grew up babysitting and working with kids. All of my jobs as a young professional involved working with kids. I couldn't wait to have some of my own!

I am also a planner. After three years of marriage, my husband and I decided to start trying. In our second month, we conceived. We were beyond excited! Seeing that stick with the word "pregnant" on it was the most incredible moment. We were going to have a baby! A little life was growing inside of me!

I wasted no time planning out everything that needed to happen to prepare for our child's birth—to-do lists, gift registry, new vehicle, research about cloth diapers and carseats, etc. Our home was a flurry of happy preparations for the new arrival.

April 11, 2014

I got a new car today! We have been looking for an SUV this week because I don't think the Ford Escort that I've been driving for the last eleven years is very safe for a car seat. Today we bought a Nissan Rogue, and I love it!

    Yes, this entry is dated exactly one week after we found out that I was pregnant. Like I said, I'm a planner! We also picked out our boy and girl baby names that same week. Excited much?

April 14, 2014

    I still don't have very many of the early pregnancy symptoms—no morning sickness or cravings, I just have to go to the bathroom frequently, and I've almost grown a cup size already. That will take some getting used to, LOL!

April 16, 2014

    We bought a crib on Craigslist today and set it up in the nursery. I know it's early, but I love seeing it in there :)

    Yes, we set the crib up in the nursery only twelve days after finding out that I was pregnant. I may have been a tad bit over-enthusiastic. Actually, no, I don't think it's possible to be over-enthusiastic when a new baby is involved.

And yes, we bought our crib on Craigslist. I love a good bargain, and shopping for something new at a store is always my last resort. We have had a lot of good experiences with Craigslist, but the crib was an adventure.

We went to pick it up in a very sketchy neighborhood. The guy who sold it to us knew nothing about it and said that it was his girlfriend's and she had left it there. I'm not sure that she even knew he was selling it, but it was a quality crib at a great price, and it ended up in our nursery. To this day, Nathan still says he can't believe we did that!

My birthday was April nineteenth, and Nathan and I went to a bed and breakfast to celebrate. It was the most wonderful place that had a little farm with chickens, sheep, pigs, donkeys, horses, and vegetable gardens. All of the food served at breakfast was grown on the property. We went fishing in the little pond, took a trail ride on horseback, and wandered around the beautiful grounds. The weather was gorgeous, and all of the flowers were in bloom against the bright green growth of spring. Best of all, Nathan and I shared a secret—a hidden life developing inside of me. Our little baby! The weekend was the perfect way to celebrate.

Before we left, I was lying in the hammock, looking up at the sky in awe and humble gratitude. I

Did you know?

Pomegranates are a symbol of fruitfulness and fertility in almost every ancient culture because of its many seeds.

grabbed my phone and took a picture of my view from the hammock—great big protective oak tree limbs stretching over me and beyond them a brilliantly blue sky, accented with puffy white clouds.

I remember thinking to myself, 'I am going to take this picture so that I can remember how perfect this exact moment is. It doesn't get any better than this.'

I look back at that picture all the time. What a blissfully innocent moment!

April 22, 2014

I spotted a little today and kind of freaked out. I did some blood work at the hospital, and they said everything looks great. It turns out that since I am irregular, I am probably only five and a half weeks pregnant instead of seven and a half, making it implantation spotting.

We have an ultrasound on Thursday so we can know for sure. Keeping calm and praying a lot. I know we can always try again, but I want THIS one!

I was already so in love with my little baby!

April 24, 2014

Everything looked good at our first appointment this morning. They bumped the due date from Dec. 7

EXCITEMENT

to Dec. 19. As suspected, I am only six weeks along. This is going to be the longest pregnancy ever! We had the ultrasound to check and make sure everything was okay with the baby.

It was so amazing! It was so small, like the size of a grain of rice, just a little line on the screen! It was too early to hear the heartbeat, but you could see a little flicker, like a tiny flashing light, and it was the heartbeat!

I can't believe there is really a tiny human growing inside me! We will go back for another ultrasound in ten days to try to hear the heartbeat again, but in the meantime I am feeling confident that all is well.

April 26, 2014

Today we had Nathan's family and my family over for lunch and badminton at our house under the pretense of my birthday get-together. After we served cake, we told them that we were pregnant, and everyone was so excited! They all just screamed! I was so excited to tell them that my hands were shaking. My mom was so happy, she cried. Then we sat around talking and making plans—it was a perfect afternoon filled with joy and anticipation.

Nathan and I both come from close families that all live in town, and sharing the news with them was such a fun event! I remember trying to get them all into the same place at the same time so that we could share the news. We finally thought that we had everyone gathered together when we were singing and cutting the cake, but right after we made the big announcement, my brother walked out of the bathroom. Oh, well!

    At our wedding, my husband and I had an idea to paint a picture together instead of doing a unity candle. Yes, I painted. During the ceremony. In my wedding dress. It was one of our favorite parts of the day, and we have the painting hanging in our living room.

    My husband and I decided to paint another picture and make a video of the process to announce on social media that we were expecting. That week we painted our picture while my brother filmed it, and we spent the weekend editing it together. Then we hung the original painting up in the nursery, right over the crib. In the video, the song that we played while we were painting was "Beautiful Things" by Gungor, the same song that we had painted with during our wedding ceremony. Only in retrospect did we realize just how appropriate the lyrics of the song truly were.

> All this pain
> I wonder if I'll ever find my way
> I wonder if my life could really change, at all
> All this earth
> Could all that is lost ever be found?
> Could a garden come out from this ground, at all?

EXCITEMENT

You make beautiful things
You make beautiful things out of the dust
You make beautiful things
You make beautiful things out of us

All around,
Hope is springing up from this old ground
Out of chaos life is being found, in you

You make me new,
You are making me new[1]

    The following Sunday at church, the director of the local pregnancy center came and spoke about their ministry to mothers who are uncertain about continuing their pregnancies and the ways that people could get involved. She had a table set up with life-size models of what a baby looks like at different stages of pregnancy.

    Nathan and I stood in front of the model of the nine-week-old fetus in wonder. It was so small, the size of a lima bean, and yet it had all of its little body parts. We smiled to each other in awe that the baby inside of me looked just like that.

    The next milestone was our nine-week ultrasound. I couldn't wait to see how our little grain of rice had grown over the past three weeks. They were running behind schedule at the doctor's office, and we sat in the waiting room for over an hour, watching the fish circle the aquarium in the center of the lobby. My husband and I held hands, looking around at all the other pregnant

---

[1] Gungor. Lyrics to "Beautiful Things." Capital Christian Music Group.

women in the lobby and wondering whether my belly would ever get that big. Finally, it was our turn to take another peek at our little baby.

TWO

SHOCK

"When I heard this, I tore my cloak and my shirt, pulled hair from my head and beard, and sat down utterly shocked."

Ezra 9:3 (NLT)

May 5, 2014

    Today we had our second ultrasound so that we could hear the heartbeat. Just seeing that little baby again made me smile and laugh. It had grown a little since the last one, and you could make out the head and body. The nurse wasn't seeing a heartbeat, though. So we tried again vaginally.

    "Sometimes, when it's this early, we have a hard time finding the heartbeat from the front," the nurse explained. She had me change into a gown so we could try again vaginally.
    As I was changing, I chatted casually with my husband, but I had this trace of worry in my mind. I didn't say it out loud, but I hoped everything was okay. Back on the table, I held my breath as the lab tech tried again. We looked expectantly at the screen, waiting to see that little flash of the heartbeat. I started to think that something may not be right. She found the fetus. There was no flashing.
    "I'm sorry," she said, "there is no heartbeat."

    No heartbeat. My worst fears were true. The baby was dead.

    Time stopped. It felt as though my heart had stopped as well. The floor seemed to drop out from under me. I reached for Nathan's hand, and my eyes filled with tears.

The lab tech took a few pictures and measurements as the tears silently rolled down my face. This was the only time I have ever seen my husband tear up in his life.

He gave me a hug and said, "We can try again." I nodded, but I couldn't speak.

I cried, Nathan held me. There is no fight at this point, only surrender.

They were still running behind schedule with the ultrasound appointments and needed the room for the next person. I changed back into my clothes, and we went to sit in the doctor's office. As we sat waiting in the leather chairs, I was completely shell-shocked.

I looked at the family pictures on the doctor's wall; him, his wife, and their huge family of children. How many kids did they have? Six? Eight? They were all smiling at me from the gold picture frame. Would I ever have a family picture like that?

The doctor came in after a few minutes. He explained that miscarriages happen all the time. He and his wife had experienced a miscarriage before their first child, too. Sometimes, if there is something wrong with the baby, the body naturally aborts it. It is very common.

I had experienced what they call a "missed miscarriage." It means that the baby's heart stops beating, but the body continues to hold the fetus because it has not recognized the loss yet. Hormonally and physically, the body continues to act as though it is pregnant and can continue to hold the baby for several more weeks. We had some options. We could wait for the body to expel the baby naturally, or we could schedule a D&C right then, and they would extract the tissue surgically.

My mind was trying to keep up. The tissue? No, that's my child! I came in to see an ultrasound of my baby, and you want to have surgery to suck it out of me right now? No! I decided to wait.

The doctor explained that waiting was psychologically and emotionally difficult for most women because there is no way to know when the body will decide to finish the process. It could be that day, or it could last for weeks, which might cause harmful infections. He told me to call and schedule the D&C if I changed my mind or call to schedule a follow-up after the miscarriage completed naturally.

If there is one thing that people have no control over, it is pregnancy. We have to leave that to God, and He is still all-knowing, faithful, and loving. The good thing is that we know everything works—we can conceive. So now it's just a matter of time—we will try again. Nathan and I spent the day together trying to figure out... what do we do now? We had sushi and hibachi and went swimming at the gym.

My husband and I left the office in a fog. Nathan called in to work to let them know he would be out for the day. We went to lunch together at a sushi place. We haven't been back to eat there since.

I just remember continually asking him, "What do we do now?" There wasn't a clear answer. There was nothing we could do. It was done. I am the 'can do' sort of person who believes that if there's a will, there's a way. But there was nothing that could change what had already happened. It was finished.

I felt like a balloon. Emotionally, I had been so excited about the new baby, filled with so many ideas, projects, and preparations. My secret baby Pinterest boards were overflowing! I had been inflated with joy almost to bursting! Suddenly, it was as if someone had let go of the end of the balloon. All of the air rushed out, leaving behind a flat and deflated shell. Balloons never look the same after being inflated and then deflated again. They get those wrinkly stretch lines that show the wear of the experience. My soul felt like that limp and wrinkled balloon.

My next question was whether it could have been my fault. I was sure that it couldn't be my fault! I had done everything right. I had followed the letter of the law when it came to every piece of literature I could get my hands on about pregnancy. I didn't eat sushi or deli meat or ride a bike. But I had ridden a horse! Could that have caused this? Even though I knew that nothing I had done had caused the miscarriage, my mind was working against me. I couldn't emotionally handle any responsibility or guilt on top of the grief I was already processing.

Sometime during our lunch, my husband did say, "Let's plan a trip." We love to travel together. He pulled out his phone and scrolled through different options. I remember being afraid to book a trip, because who knew? Maybe we would get pregnant again next month! He reasoned that we could plan it for five or six months from then and still be able to go even if I did get pregnant. We booked a two-week trip to China then and there. It seemed like a strange thing to do, but I have to give my husband credit for his foresight—I'm so glad that we did.

I don't remember going to the gym to swim that day, but it doesn't surprise me. I was on the swim team in high school, and there is something very calming about getting into the perfect rhythm of strokes and breathing, following the line at the bottom of the pool, and counting laps.

Did you know?

Each pomegranate supposedly contains 613 seeds, the same number of laws in the Old Testament. For this reason, it is a food traditionally eaten at Rosh Hashana.

After all these years, I remember two other things from that day. The first is that someone stole our circular saw. Between my husband and I, we are always creating something. I had been working on a project that morning and left the saw in the carport while we went to the appointment, assuming that I would finish when we got back. When we got home, the saw was gone. Someone had taken it right out from under our carport! I felt so violated. I remember thinking, 'That isn't the only thing that was taken from me today.' It was also

SHOCK

somewhat symbolic because it would be months before I would have the will to work on any project.

I did go in to work for a while; I wanted to see the kids.

The second thing I remember is going to work. At the time I was the elementary director at an after-school program for at-risk kids. It wasn't the kind of job I could just call in sick for, so I went to work that afternoon. Work would turn out to be a life-saver over the next few months. I didn't know it at the time, but working with the kids would ironically be the only time that I could stop thinking about the child that I lost.

We let our families know.

Women do not often talk about miscarriage, because it is such a dark, heavy, and deeply personal topic. We are always told to wait until we are twelve weeks pregnant to share the news because there may be a miscarriage. Here's my question: so what? Why should I be expected to mourn the loss of my baby in private? Why are we expected to feel shame in our culture when pregnancy loss occurs? Why all of this secrecy? I am so grateful that I had told my family that we were pregnant before the miscarriage happened!
I would not have wanted to tell my mother, 'I was

pregnant, but I had a miscarriage.' That would have been a lot for her to process at once before being able to show empathy in my grief. It was really nice to be able to rejoice with all of our family and friends for a time, and then let them share in the loss as well. But this is rarely the case. Most women who experience a miscarriage have only shared the pregnancy news with their spouse, because most miscarriages happen so early. That feeling of struggling alone is what makes processing the grief of miscarriage so difficult.

Having a miscarriage is often a very lonely road to travel. Even those closest to us, like our husbands, will be sympathetic but will not fully understand or experience the same emotions that we are going through. It is easy to feel as though we are the only one in the world without a baby, but we're not. So many women are experiencing the same emotional and physical roller coaster we are, but no one talks about it.

Now we wait for the miscarriage to actually happen, for my body to act on what my mind already knows. They say it can take up to six weeks before it happens naturally, but I want to avoid the surgery if possible. I'm afraid that as hard as today was, the next part may be the hardest. And yet, God has covered me with His grace today and carried me with His peace. I know His will and timing are best, and I will rest in that.

Life was continuing on as normal all around me,

but inside, I was standing still. This was the beginning of one of the most difficult seasons of life that I have had to walk through.

Shock and denial go hand-in-hand. At first this took the form of a hypothetical denial: 'I just can't believe that this happened to me!' But within twenty-four hours, it turned into a literal denial, thanks to Google. I made a classic mistake the week we got the news. I Googled. I searched the internet for information on missed miscarriages: how long it would take to expel the tissue afterwards, what the recovery would be like, how long we should wait before we tried to get pregnant again, and stories of other women in similar circumstances.

may 9, 2014

Today was a rough day. I had been accepting things pretty well, letting it consume my thoughts a little less each day until I had a realization today. For the first time, I wondered... can they misdiagnose a missed miscarriage? I Googled it—that was a mistake.

In my reading, I came across some unbelievable stories of women who were diagnosed with a missed miscarriage, but the doctor had been wrong! Their babies were healthy and living, and the heartbeat had been there all along, undetected!

There is an entire website of stories of misdiagnoses with ultrasounds of no heartbeat, only to show a perfectly healthy baby a few weeks later. Suddenly there was hope, and I wanted a second opinion.

My mind started reeling. What if my baby is fine? Can I get a second opinion? Can we try to find the heartbeat again? How can I make sure? I couldn't sleep as the possibility of life haunted me. I was determined not to get a D&C because I might actually be hurting a perfectly fine baby! These thoughts consumed me for several days, and I thought I might, quite literally, go crazy with uncertainty. The rational part of my brain knew that this was all ridiculous. But let me just say that the pregnancy hormones were still raging, and my poor body was so confused. Was I growing a baby or not?

In my distress, I needed someone to talk to, and I did something very strange—I called the local pregnancy center. Maybe it was because the director had spoken at our church just a week before, and she was on my mind, but I knew I needed someone in the field to be the voice of reason.

I felt so silly when I called: "I was pregnant and had a missed miscarriage this week, and I know you usually talk to women who are pregnant but don't want to be, and not women who wish they were pregnant… but, um, I just really need someone to talk to about all of this…" and that was as far as I got before sobbing.

The director was so nice. She helped bring me

back to the reality that the miscarriage really had happened, but reminded me that God's promises were still true. She prayed for me, and I felt God's peace and reassurance.

But at the same time I knew that the baby was gone and all that was left in me was a shell. Welcome to the denial and bargaining stages of grief! Finally accepting the truth again was like hearing the news all over again. I feel like I am back at square one emotionally, and I am praying that the miscarriage will start soon just so that I can have some closure.

Once again, I came to terms with the fact that I did not have a living baby inside of me. That day I also started financially supporting the pregnancy center on a monthly basis.

It seems like after I had my miscarriage, almost everyone I did share the news with had experienced a miscarriage at some point as well. Their stories made me realize that I was far from alone in my experience— women who had fourteen miscarriages in a row, lost their baby at full term, or who had multiple miscarriages and stillborn children. While I was tempted to believe that my loss and grief was not as significant in comparison to theirs, I quickly realized that there is no scale of one to ten when it comes to grief. Every loss is significant. Talking to women who had not only lived through such tragedies, but could also praise God for

His provision in the midst of them, was such a huge help for me. This is something we need to talk more about.

While I valued wise counsel, I also received a lot of unsolicited and well-meaning responses from other voices. In the shock phase, these attempts to comfort me weren't any consolation. With the loss so recent, almost every comment caused offense or pain. And for every piece of optimistic encouragement that someone offered, my resentment had a defensive retort:

> "There are three needs of the griever: To find the words for the loss, to say the words aloud and to know that the words have been heard."
> - Victoria Alexander

"A lot of times when the body naturally miscarries, it's because there was something wrong with the baby, so it's really a blessing in disguise."
No, it's not a blessing. Not under any circumstances is this, or will this ever be, a blessing.

"It just wasn't meant to be."
God very intentionally created this child, so yes, my baby was meant to be.

"You will be able to try again!"
Yes, we will, and it won't magically reverse the fact that we lost a baby.

"At least you know you can get pregnant."

I'm not sure what good that is if I can't carry the baby to term.

"I had a miscarriage, but look! Now I have three beautiful children!"
That's wonderful, but I don't know that that will be the end of my story.

"God knows best, and His timing is perfect."
I know that's true, but it doesn't comfort me in the raw experience of grief.

At this point in my journey, I interpreted their efforts to comfort me as a thinly-veiled attempt to dismiss the gravity of my pain. They were trying to make me feel better, but the truth was that I didn't want to feel better for a long time. The right word of wisdom wasn't what I needed in this stage, anyway. What I needed was for someone to acknowledge the legitimacy and depth of my pain and allow me to feel it fully for a while.

I wanted to feel all of the loss, the sorrow, and the grief. I wanted to fully experience the pain because it was sad. The life of the child that I loved was lost. Ultimately, I felt like feeling better would mean I was forgetting my child.

THREE

APPREHENSION

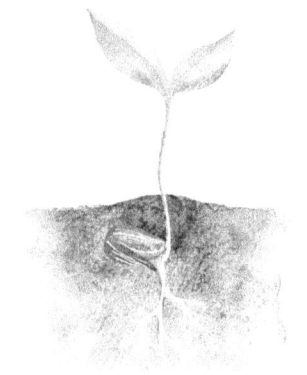

*"What I feared has come upon me;
what I dreaded has happened to me.
I have no peace, no quietness;
I have no rest, but only turmoil."*

Job 3:25-26 (NIV)

Once I recovered from the shock, I was filled with anticipation as I waited for the miscarriage to actually occur. When would I expel the tissue? What if it happened at work, in front of all the kids? That would be difficult to explain. What if it happened at church? Or the grocery store? I started bringing heavy pads and an extra change of clothes in my car everywhere I went, just in case.

What would it feel like? Would it be painful? The doctor said I would experience cramping as though it were a usual menstrual period. But I have a male doctor—he hasn't ever had a miscarriage or a menstrual period! How does he know? How long would it be until it happened? Would it be days? Or weeks? How long would it take to finish? Would it be very sudden? Or gradual? Basically, I was driving myself crazy while waiting for the inevitable. The fear of the unknown was overwhelming.

May 10, 2014

I started spotting today, and it was a feeling of relief. God is so gracious!

I was so relieved that it started on a Saturday, when I was home, instead of at work. I was also relieved that some of the unknown questions would soon have closure. I was ready for the physical miscarriage to finally be over so that I could move on.

May 11, 2014

    Mother's Day. So many hopes and dreams feel empty and lost today.

    On Mother's Day, I was carrying a lifeless fetus inside me. I thought I would never make it through that day. The pain was so raw and the loss so substantial. On the way to church that morning, I so desperately wanted Nathan to tell me, 'Happy Mother's Day,' to legitimize the fact that something real had happened! But at the same time, I was so afraid that he might say something, and I would break into a thousand pieces and never recover.

    Poor guy—what a lose-lose situation. He didn't say anything, but when we got to church, a friend gave me a hug and said it. I went to the bathroom and cried my eyes out and missed all the music.

    Just a side note—if you have had a miscarriage, you have the right to celebrate or not celebrate Mother's Day. You are a mother. You will always be a mother. And you have lost a child.

May 16, 2014

    The miscarriage actually happened today. I took the day off of work because of the pain. Over the last few days it has been like a heavy period, but today I had about three hours of really intense cramping (two Advil didn't even touch the pain). Lots of blood, and then the worst was over.

Of all of the not helpful comments that I received in the shock phase, there was one that I actually listened to and used. It came from my sister-in-law, who had struggled with infertility for years.

She simply told me, "Chocolate helps." She was right.

I remember a few things about the day that I actually miscarried the baby. First, the pain was much worse than a regular menstrual period, and I spent a lot of time silently cursing my doctor for not preparing me better. Secondly, I remember going through a whole box of Thin Mints, crying in pain on the sofa. I spent most of the day curled up in the fetal position, experiencing intense pain, wondering if that was what labor felt like. If so, I was pretty sure that I would never be able to give birth should I ever get the chance. After changing out a ridiculous number of pads, I finally just sat on the toilet for the worst of it, and that helped.

I knew exactly when the baby passed. Even with the baby only at nine weeks old, I could feel when it came out. I struggled for a moment, trying to decide if I should look or not. Did I want to see my baby? I knew that I would never be able to unsee it.

We had pet rabbits at the time, and they gave birth every few months. It is common for rabbits to push a sickly baby out of the nesting box and reject it. Several months before, our rabbit had pushed an entire litter of babies out of the nesting box. They were only a day or two old, and by the time we found them they had died in the winter air. They were so small, only a little bigger than my thumbnail. At the time, I had cried in shock and horror at the sight.

Sitting on the toilet, I thought about those little baby rabbits. Instead of looking, I closed my eyes and flushed. And then, I cried.

Once again, I had a feeling of relief, a sense of closure. I am not yet at the point where I am looking forward to trying again or thinking of the next baby, still missing this one. The next step is to have another ultrasound to see that all the uterus has emptied. (Do I need a visual of my empty womb?)

May 28, 2014

Today was my ultrasound to check and make sure that everything has cleared out of my uterus and the miscarriage was complete. Even though I have been doing much better this week, just walking into the waiting room made me want to cry, and then seeing my empty uterus was just so different from the last time, looking at a tiny life.

Sitting in the waiting room that day was torture. I was watching the same fish circling in the tank as I had just a few weeks ago, filled with such joy, hope, and promise. I was surrounded by pregnant women in the lobby once again, blooming with new life. But I was empty. I had no life in me. No hope. No growth. I had loss.

However, everything looked good, and the nurse said that if a miscarriage has to happen, I had had the "best scenario." She said the ovaries and uterus lining were very healthy, and we shouldn't have any trouble conceiving again.

I have always been a very positive person, definitely a glass half-full kind of girl. Even in this journal entry, I make an effort to see the best in each part of the situation and count my blessings. We wouldn't need to do surgery, and I presumably would be able to conceive again. Life would move on.

I asked her for the picture from my last ultrasound, and she printed it for me. Even though it is just a tiny blip on the screen, it is the only tangible remembrance that we have of our first child. Leaving the office, once again, I was fighting back tears. The grief isn't missing a lost loved one, it's just feeling a loss, an unexplainable emptiness, the grief of a dream unfulfilled.

It was difficult to put into words what I was mourning at that point. I had never met my child, so

I couldn't miss his or her personality. While it would seem that this distinction would make the loss feel less significant, it actually had the opposite effect. It felt less like a loss and more like a violation. I felt like something had been unfairly taken from me. I felt robbed and cheated out of the joy and hope that I should have been experiencing.

Undated

    30 Days of Choosing Gratitude
    Gratitude: learning to recognize and express appreciation for the benefits we have received from God and others.
    I know I've been greatly blessed, but I don't often stop to actually express my gratitude to God.
    Father, I want to spend the next 30 days intentionally thanking you for all of your blessings. Thank you for a new day with the kids at Bridge, and the opportunity to show them life with you. Thank you for the sacrifice you made in giving your Son and that you share in our pain when we also experience loss.

    This was a great idea! How better to choose joy in the midst of sorrow than to start with gratitude. Thirty days of writing down all of the things that I was grateful for would help me focus on God's blessings, rather than on the one thing that I was missing. As you will see with my next journal entry, this great idea never made it past day one. But I guess one day of gratitude is better than none. Moving on.

    I have always used writing as a personal way to process thoughts, emotions, ideas, and life lessons. When I write, I pour out my heart to God. While I often begin from a place of confusion, I end in a place of peace. God meets me in the writing process, speaks truth to my heart, and brings my mind in alignment with His promises. Therefore, when I am avoiding God, I avoid writing as well.

    In this season, I stopped journaling. What followed was two months of silence. Silence in which I didn't want to hear God's voice, because I was afraid of what He might say. Silence in which I tried to numb the pain, rather than deal with it. Silence in which I wallowed in self-pity and didn't want to stop being the victim. I wasn't in a healthy place, but I also wasn't ready to do the growing up it would take to become healthy.

FOUR

EMOTIONAL INSTABILITY

"It's so curious: one can resist tears and 'behave' very well in the hardest hours of grief. But then someone makes you a friendly sign behind a window, or one notices that a flower that was in bud only yesterday has suddenly blossomed, or a letter slips from a drawer… and everything collapses."

— Colette

I know you don't know me, although you are getting to know me quite intimately in these pages. The problem is that the 'me' that you are getting to know is quite different from my typical self. When not walking through grief, I am not a crier. I am a content person, even-tempered, a peace-maker, predictable, trustworthy, responsible, goal-oriented, motivated, and self-disciplined. I value order, rational thinking, planning, and positivity.

If you knew me, you would not recognize me as I describe myself over the months that followed. To sum them up in one word, they were emotional. I was an unpredictable basket-case, a roller coaster of craziness. I was filled with frustration, confusion, anger, sadness, and emptiness. I had lost myself, and I missed myself, but I didn't know where I had gone or how to get me back.

I was angry with myself because I was experiencing a change in behavior that was strange to me—a lack of desire to do anything, no motivation or joy in life, uncontrollable mood swings (with lots of tears), and a new habit of forgetfulness. None of these were my usual characteristics, and seeing them made me feel too broken and incompetent to deal with the usual stressors of the everyday.

❦ BITTER SORROW ❦

I never fully understood the depth of the word 'devastation' until I had a miscarriage. I was utterly devastated, almost paralyzed by sorrow. The smallest things would make me cry. So. Many. Tears. Just when I would think that I was doing better, the strangest, smallest, most inconspicuous occurrence would set off an emotional release of epic proportions. Why couldn't I keep myself from crying? It made me feel a little better to blame the crazy amounts of confused hormones in my body.

When I would try to keep the pain away, it would follow me into my dreams! One night, I dreamed that I was walking along a road and saw a bird's nest in a tree with a mother bird sitting on three eggs. The nest fell out of the tree, and the eggs broke on the ground. Immediately, I fell to my knees with heaving sobs, crying uncontrollably. It was the kind of sobbing that comes from the stomach, and I couldn't breathe. Everyone around was looking at me like I was crazy for crying over such a small thing. I woke up with that renewed feeling that I get after a really good cry. I guess I needed it.

Eventually, I was able to stop feeling ashamed of the tears and accept them. When I would see yet another baby announcement on Facebook, and I wanted to throw my laptop out a window, I told myself it was okay. When I saw a newborn in the grocery store and started crying hysterically in the middle of aisle nine, it was okay. When everyone around me seemed to be progressing in life, and I was standing still, it was okay. I gave myself permission to cry a little every day, I just didn't let myself stay there.

I remember a friend calling me to catch up. We talked for fifteen minutes about her life, just like normal.

When she asked me how I was doing, I opened my mouth to say that I was fine. What came out instead, were huge sobs. I ugly cried into the phone, making incomprehensible attempts at speech for a while, until I finally hung up.

One Sunday at church, my pastor was preaching on grief and enduring hardships. He made a statement that when we go through trials, it draws us closer to God. He said that on the other side, we would value the intimate relationship with God that developed as a result so much, that the trial would be worth it. He claimed that we would not want to change those circumstances even if we could. I remember thinking, 'I will never feel that way about this situation. I will never not want to reverse what has happened.' I couldn't imagine it at the time, but he would turn out to be right.

FRUSTRATION

I was frustrated with my body. I kept on bleeding, and my cycles were not returning to normal. How could I get pregnant again if I still wasn't ovulating? I felt stuck—like life was moving forward all around me, but I was watching from the outside. Friends who had been pregnant at the same time as me began posting baby pictures on social media. Other friends announced new pregnancies. I was so happy for them, but wondered why I was being denied what they had been granted. Each day was a new struggle.

I was also frustrated with my mind. At work, I was doing things that were completely uncharacteristic of me. On several occasions, I missed meetings. It's not that I was late or decided not to go. I completely forgot that they were ever supposed to happen. Each time, I was shocked, after the fact, when I realized that I hadn't been there, and I was angry with myself for not remembering. It almost felt as if my mind was rebelling against me by taking information that I needed and purposefully tossing it out of my memory. I had never experienced anything like it before. I had no explanation whatsoever for my behavior.

    This mutiny of the mind seemed to permeate other areas of life as well. Even the simplest tasks seemed overwhelming. Getting the oil in my car changed, going to the dentist for a regular cleaning, or paying a routine bill all seemed like insurmountable tasks that I couldn't handle. I knew that these small things shouldn't be so stressful. It was frustrating to not be able to function at my usual level of competence and to not fully know what had changed or how to fix it.

ENVIOUS ANGER

    The anger began even before I had completed the miscarriage, and it was a jealous anger. I went to a nephew's birthday party while I was still carrying the baby with no heartbeat, and there was a lady there with her three-week-old, beautiful baby. I'm pretty sure that if my eyes had been laserbeams, that baby would have exploded into a ball of flames.

    People who hardly knew me would ask with a sly smile when Nathan and I were planning on starting a family. It wasn't their fault, but people would always seem to ask or comment on the most inopportune days. Although, when the grief is recent, there are really no good days to talk about it.

The same week as the devastating ultrasound, while I was still carrying the baby, I was making photocopies at church when a former coworker playfully asked me when Nathan and I were going to start having kids. In my mind, I gave some evasive and witty answer. In reality, I honestly don't remember how I responded. I do remember turning back to the copier and trying to look busy to hide the fact that I was visibly falling apart. Thankfully, she wasn't stopping around for a long conversation and scurried back to her desk. The buttons on the copier blurred as my eyes filled with tears. I rested my shaking hands on the plastic cover of the machine as it hummed and spat out paper after paper. Only God knew if or when we would have kids.

My relationships with others became strained. Friendship with anyone pregnant or who had a baby was an exceptional struggle. A good friend of mine wanted to have lunch, and since we hadn't seen each other in several years, I just knew she was going to tell me that she was pregnant. The whole way driving to meet her, I was physically sick to my stomach at the thought of one more person's joyous news. She wasn't pregnant, thank goodness! Then, I felt guilty for feeling that way, beating myself up for not being willing to celebrate with her over her hypothetical news.

This anger continued throughout the process of grieving. Four of my five closest friends were pregnant at the time. As their pregnancies progressed, and their due dates arrived, I spoke to them less and less. It wasn't anything that they had said or done, I simply couldn't face the reality of what my life would have looked like. Seeing their growing children is still a reminder of what age my child would have been.

I was angry with any discussions about abortion. I was incensed that anyone would want to destroy the life that I so desperately wanted to experience. I had an acute lack of empathy for moms complaining about how their baby had kept them up all night. If someone was experiencing any uncomfortable pregnancy symptoms and wanted a listening ear, they always regretted sharing with me.

> **❝** Grief, I've learned, is really just love. It's all the love you want to give but cannot give.... All of that unspent love gathers up in the corners of your eyes and in that part of your chest that gets that hollow feeling. The happiness of love turns to sadness when unspent. Grief is just love with no place to go. **❞**
> - Jamie Anderson

At the time, I worked with a lot of low-income families and at-risk children, where I encountered many young, unmarried mothers struggling to provide for their families. When one would announce a new pregnancy, rather than feeling sympathy for their difficult circumstances, I couldn't help but turn to God and think, 'Really? Why them, and not me?'

In my mind, this thinking seemed justified. Looking back now, I am appalled at my arrogance.

EMPTINESS

During these months, I also lacked my usual spark of creativity and gusto for starting new projects. While I was usually brimming with ideas, I was empty. There was no motivation, no energy, no desire. I simply had nothing in me to give. However, I still had to fill my time.

People turn to all kinds of distractions when dealing with grief. These distractions can easily turn into addictions to food, drugs, alcohol, relationships, media, etc. My own addiction is something that I'm not proud of, and looking back, I realize how ridiculous it was.

Are you ready for this confession? I played Farmville 2.

Okay, I know that's not what you were expecting to hear. I doubt it shows up on many lists of common grief addictions, but I'm just being honest.

Farmville is a game on the phone in which you have a virtual farm, and you earn points to plant new crops, add new animals, and slowly grow your garden. It is a repetitive and pointless game—very addictive and very time-consuming.

I can't tell you how many hours I spent playing that game. Any opportunity to be alone with my thoughts was quickly eliminated by pulling out my phone. I blocked reality with the screen in the palm of my hand. It sounds so dumb now looking back. I guess I could have drowned my sorrows in an addiction with much greater consequences than simply wasting time. Although, what commodity is more precious and limited than time?

My media black hole swallowed up hours and hours a day, for months, where I could exist in a virtual reality, in which the pain didn't exist. It was a comforting place to retreat, where I felt safe. Thankfully, I didn't stay there forever.

During this season of grief, I was not acting wisely. Looking back at my actions brings to mind the definition of wisdom laid out in the book of James.

> Who is wise and understanding among you? Let them show it by their good life, by deeds done in the humility that comes from wisdom. But if you harbor bitter envy and selfish ambition in your hearts, do not boast about it or deny the truth. Such "wisdom" does not come down from heaven but is earthly, unspiritual, demonic. For where you have envy and selfish ambition, there you find disorder and every evil practice. But the wisdom that comes from heaven is first of all pure; then peace-loving, considerate, submissive, full of mercy and good fruit, impartial and sincere. Peacemakers who sow in peace reap a harvest of righteousness.
> James 3:13-18 (NIV)

When looking at the list of traits displayed by God's wisdom and those displayed by the world's wisdom, it is pretty obvious that my actions and emotions were led by the world's wisdom. At the time, I thought that I was justified in feeling and acting that way because of my pain, but it was just an excuse. I was avoiding God, avoiding His Word, and allowing Satan to have free rein with my emotions.

The results were exactly what the verses in James describe: bitter envy of those who had what I did not, the selfish ambition of wanting my will done in my timing, and a life that was earthly, unspiritual, and full of disorder. The negative emotions that I had allowed to rein in my heart for so long were a season in my grief process. I often wonder if that time period of emotional instability was a necessary piece that I had to work through or if it could have been avoided. In either case, my bitter sorrow, frustration, envious anger, and emptiness were a product of sin, a result of Satan's influence over my heart and mind. Many people will say that there is no wrong way to grieve, but the Bible gives a clear warning against turning to earthly wisdom over God's wisdom, even in our despair.

I wish that I had embraced His wisdom in this season and experienced the character promised in scripture—pure, peace-loving, sincere, and full of mercy and every good fruit. However, notice in this list that all of these good results are related to how we deal with others, rather than blessings for ourselves. Being full of mercy implies being merciful to others who are insensitive to our pain. Sincerity means being honest with others about our struggles. Being peace-loving demonstrates how we should desire to have strong relationships with others, even when they have been blessed in ways that we haven't.

This wisdom, while it would indirectly bless us, seeks to share God's blessing with others. In this stage of grief, I was far too concerned with the blessings that I felt that God was withholding from me to be able to give anything to anyone else.

Interestingly enough, the only time that I wasn't thinking about my loss was when I was at work with the kids. They were such a blessing during this season. Working with them was an outlet to freely give the love that I had so desperately wanted to share with my own child. Being with them forced me to think about someone other than myself and to deal with problems other than my own.

Only in that mindset was I able to find peace, just as the verses in James claim. Isn't it amazing how God's Word is true, even when it seems to contradict everything that makes sense in the world? In order to find peace in my grief, I had to focus on others.

During this time, Nathan and I were in a homesteading phase in which we were using our quarter-acre yard in the middle of the city to attempt to produce all of our own food. We had a large vegetable garden, chickens, rabbits, and a greenhouse, complete with an aquaponics system to raise fish. Slowly, I began to leave the virtual reality farm and re-enter the real one in our backyard.

Gardening has always been therapeutic for me, but growing food is even more satisfying. Something about digging in the dirt in the quiet of the morning, just as the sun comes up, can still the mind and heal the soul. Planting seeds, watching them sprout in time, lifting their heads from the damp soil and opening the first two green leaves up to the sun, is an amazing transformation to witness.

    The God who created these systems of growth through seasons—causing seeds to sprout, grow into mature plants, create new seeds, and die—is the same one who is the author of my own story. Knowing this gave me hope. There was so much life all around me with new litters of baby rabbits being born, chickens pecking around contentedly, and plants flourishing and bearing fruit. As I pulled weeds, planted seeds, and picked vegetables, I began to experience peace.

    While I had ignored God through writing, He followed me into the garden, and He met me there with a gentle, healing presence. It was there that I began to ask the questions that had plagued me throughout the grieving process. Not only did these questions challenge my faith, but I knew that the answers would determine my relationship with God moving forward. I never blamed God for what had happened, but I did question His will. Even more, I questioned my willingness to surrender all to follow His will.

    I started with the basic question that everyone asks when anything happens. Why? Why did this happen to me? My immediate reaction was to demand my rights. I was a good person, so I deserved to have good things. Unfortunately, I also knew that this idea was not biblical. My perspective of 'good' and 'bad' was skewed. I look at the evil around me and think that anything better than that, must be good, but God looks at His own perfection, and whatever is less than that, is flawed. The Bible says, "for all have sinned and fall short of the glory of God"

(Rom. 3:23 NIV), and "all have turned away, they have together become worthless; there is no one who does good, not even one" (Rom. 3:12 NIV).

After reading these verses, I could not be so audacious as to claim that I was a 'good' person, and I certainly couldn't claim to deserve anything based on that fictitious goodness. I was a sinful person who had been forgiven by God's grace. Since I did nothing to deserve that grace, I was not in a position to demand anything of God. Instead, I should have been taking a posture of gratitude, and I was far from that! I needed a perspective change. I needed to see things as God does, whose ways are higher than my ways, and whose thoughts are higher than my thoughts (Is. 55:9). To get the right idea about my miscarriage, I required a correct view of God, His character, and His intentions for me, which prompted my next question.

Was my miscarriage part of God's plan? Was it in His will for this to happen? Let me say something loud and clear—women having miscarriages was never God's plan! God's plan was perfect. God created Adam and Eve to live in constant companionship with Him in the Garden of Eden. The garden was a home for them that was free of sin, death, jealousy, pain, pride, illness, and tears. It was a place of perfect communion between the Creator of the universe and His creation.

Did you know?

Scholars believe that the forbidden fruit in the Garden of Eden could have been a pomegranate.

This was the plan—*this* is what God wanted to share with us forever. (Side note—Was it a coincidence that God decided to reveal this to me while I was working in a garden? I think not.)

Unfortunately, the plan went awry. Humans have free will, and Adam and Eve broke the one rule that God had given them, to not eat the fruit from the Tree of the Knowledge of Good and Evil. By eating the fruit, they choose a different path from what God had planned. Sin entered the picture, and all sin comes with consequences. The specific consequence for Eve's sin demonstrates, in my opinion, one of the greatest struggles that we have to face as women.

Genesis 3:16a says, "To the woman [God] said, 'I will make your pains in childbearing very severe; with painful labor you will give birth to children'" (NIV).

The first part of her curse is that she will have pain in childbearing. Growing up, I always believed this to be the physical pain in the actual birthing process, which is true. However, I have come to see this curse as a much more comprehensive pain that every woman experiences, whether or not she has children.

This pain could take the form of frustration over not being able to have children, the grief of losing a child before it can be born, the burden that drives some women to take the life of their child prematurely in the womb, or the weight of responsibility that comes with actually bringing another human being into existence. As all mothers can attest, the pain does not end with birth, but continues as children grow—pain when they hurt, pain when they choose not to follow God, pain when they reject the instruction and wisdom of their parents. The pain of the actual birth is only one of the many forms of this curse.

One thing in life that is unique to females, the ability to bear children, comes with an amazing bond between a mother and child. However, due to the curse of sin, this mother-child bond now comes at a price. This love for my child, this desire to have them, and this burden to care for them brings pain no matter what the circumstances are surrounding their conception, gestation, birth, and beyond. We have been cursed as a result of our own sin nature, and this is our burden to bear as women.

I wish I could blame Eve for all of this, but I know myself, and I would have eaten the fruit, too. We traded God's plan for our own, and death is the result. Romans 6:23a says, "for the wages of sin is death" (NIV). We have all chosen sin, and we have been dying ever since.

But what about the promise in Jeremiah 29:11? Is that one still true? "'For I know the plans I have for you,' declares the Lord, 'plans to prosper you and not to harm you, plans to give you hope and a future'" (NIV).

Can God still have a good plan in a fallen world? What was happening in my life didn't seem like a good plan. The amazing thing about this verse is that it is given to the Israelites as they are being sent into seventy years of captivity in Babylon. Talk about a time to question God's plan! But the seventy years are critical. The Israelites needed all seventy of those years to work through their crisis of faith in order to trust in what God had planned for them. The seventy years are where the work of sanctification takes place to make room for the redemption to follow. James 1:3-4 says, "You know that the testing of your faith produces perseverance. Let perseverance finish its work so that you may be mature and complete, not lacking anything" (NIV).

God does not promise to tell us His plan, give us a timeline for the plan, or explain Himself in the midst of working out the plan in our lives. He only promises that He has one, and that it is good! The plan we have for ourselves is not the same as God's plan for us, and His plan is infinitely better. While we choose sin and death in our selfishness and sin, God has a plan of redemption.

When Experiencing EMOTIONAL INSTABILITY

When you are experiencing frustration, sorrow, anger, and emptiness, Satan loves to jump in and pile on some guilt and shame for feeling that way. It is important to strike a balance. Choose healthy ways to process your emotions, but also offer yourself grace when you act in the world's wisdom rather than God's. Satan strives to keep us alienated from God by convincing us that when we approach Him, He will be waiting with a lightning bolt to strike us down. Contrary to what Satan wants you to believe, God is not condemning you. Instead, He is offering forgiveness, grace, and tender mercies as you wade through emotional instability.

He understands the depth of your pain and is present with you in it! He grieves with you! At some point, you will be able to emerge from emotional instability, but there is a time when the pain still permeates everything. If that is the case, you don't have to suck it up and move on. Let God sit with you and simply be present in your pain.

The first question I asked my husband after we found out was, "What do we do now?" How do we move on? It can be helpful to remember the four "R's:" remember, record, resume, and rely.

REMEMBER

If you have any momentos or physical evidence of the pregnancy (ultrasound photos, etc.), keep them in a special place to revisit as needed while you grieve. It may be helpful to keep them in a place where you go to grieve. I put our painting in the nursery with the crib, and I put our ultrasound photo in the crib as well. When I needed a moment to let myself cry, I would go in the nursery and give myself time to feel the pain of the loss. Let yourself experience the grief, and allow yourself to have an emotional release. Just don't stay there. After a little while, I would leave the nursery, close the door, and go about my day.

If you feel stuck or struggle to move on, reach out to someone. Find someone who has experienced this grief and has gotten to the other side. It may seem insensitive to bring up the topic with them, but discussing it will help both of you in your healing!

RECORD

Take some time to figure out what you have lost. This may seem simple, but in fact, it is much more complicated than you would think. This was our first child, and the list of losses to mourn was long. Obviously, we were mourning the death of a child. It was amazing how deeply we felt the loss of a child we had never even met. It felt like a piece of us had died as well. The empty hole it left was overwhelming.

You may be grieving the loss of knowing their gender, their personality, or what they would have looked like and all of the firsts you would have shared.

You know, the ones you had already thought about in your mind with each passing week of pregnancy—the first time holding them in the delivery room, first steps, first words, first day of school, learning to drive, and getting married. You are mourning all of it at once.

But you may be mourning so much more than that, as well. For me, as a first-time mother, so much hope and anticipation were wrapped up in that plastic stick that announced the news. Releasing my 'right' to be a mother, my hopes for this new life, and the plans that I had for raising him or her was just as much of a loss. I was even mourning the loss of my previous innocence to grief.

A person going through grief experiences loss on many levels, and figuring out and naming all of the elements involved can be very helpful. Use the space provided at the end of this chapter to keep a list. It may take months for you to fully put into words each loss tied to the miscarriage. I encourage you to keep adding to the list for as long as it takes. It is amazing how much healing can be found in simply putting into words the reasons for the emotions that you are experiencing. Every loss on your list is legitimate. Let yourself fully mourn each one.

Next, and this is so important, take some time to figure out what you have gained. While you are experiencing loss on so many different levels, you will also gain some things and find things to be grateful for. Be sure to make a list of those things as well. There is space at the end of this chapter to record your findings.

As this was our first pregnancy, we were grateful

to know that we could conceive. I was more grateful for life in general and did not take that gift for granted. I was extremely grateful for my amazing husband, who had been with me every step of the way, on the good and bad days, when I wasn't sure if I was crazy or sane. I was grateful for God's grace. I was grateful for His peace in the storm, reassured that this was not the end, but a step along the way. Take time to appreciate the things that you wouldn't have noticed otherwise. This list may take even longer to compose than the list of what you have lost. This is a list that you can continue to add to for years!

✿ RESUME ✿

When you are ready, look to the future. I wanted to get pregnant again as soon as possible. How better to recover from the pain than to experience the joy of new life again? However, it takes a long time to recover physically, emotionally, and mentally. Don't rush it. Know that getting pregnant again will not mean that the miscarriage never happened. There will always be a part of us that loves our child and misses them. The progression to healing will be slow—a few steps forward and a few steps back, but it will come.

✿ RELY ✿

Don't turn away from God in the season that you need Him most. It may take a while to come to terms with what you believe. I avoided spending time in the Bible for a long time, and my prayers would vacillate between being deep and vulnerable to being shallow and superficial. Don't make the mistake that I did of choosing my own wisdom over God's wisdom. Even if you are struggling spiritually, don't close out the One who does truly understand how you are feeling and has the power to give you peace in the midst of it. He does have a good plan for you, and He will carry you through this difficult time to show you what He has next.

    Reading about the answers I found to my own spiritual questions is not going to satisfy your desire for a response from God. You are going to have to do the difficult work of muddling through the crisis of faith at your own pace and in your own way, just as I did. You are going to have to open God's Word and allow it to become living and active for you (Heb. 4:12). Until God showed me the answers Himself, I was not ready to rely on them, and I am sure that it will be the same for you.

What I Have Lost

What I Have Lost

What I Have Gained

What I Have Gained

FIVE

HONESTY

"You never know how much you really believe anything until its truth or falsehood becomes a matter of life and death to you. It is easy to say you believe a rope to be strong and sound as long as you are merely using it to cord a box. But suppose you had to hang by that rope over a precipice. Wouldn't you then first discover how much you really trusted it?"

— *C. S. Lewis, A Grief Observed*

July 27, 2014

    I've been avoiding you, Father. Maybe because I don't know what to say or what questions to ask, or maybe because I don't really want to know the answers. I keep coming back to the same question—Is Jesus really all I need? If my priorities are correct, and I am truly a Christian, then Jesus is all I need, and everything else is just extra. I thought this was true in my life until this loss.

    If I can never have children (which I don't think is the case, but for the sake of conversation), am I okay with that because I have Jesus? If something happens to Nathan or my family, can I release them through Jesus? If my job ends, the house is destroyed, reputation ruined, would Jesus be enough for me?

    This question: Is Jesus enough? Is He my all? It is not *a* question, it is *the* question. The answer to this question is everything. My entire purpose, existence, and salvation are wrapped up in the answer to this question. It is a question that I will face over and over as my life circumstances change.

    The problem with this question is that I can never truly be sure of my answer. Why? Because I have so many blessings that I cannot possibly ever come to the end of them and know that I would still choose Jesus over them. Even Job in the Bible, who lost so many crucial pieces of his life, did not lose everything. Don't we serve a good God, who has blessed us so immensely that we will never truly know our answer to this question?

In order to finally believe that Jesus is enough, I had to get an accurate understanding of God's character. Who could give me a more complete description of God's character than God?

> The Lord, the Lord,
> the compassionate and gracious God,
> slow to anger, abounding in love and
> faithfulness, maintaining love to thousands,
> and forgiving wickedness, rebellion and sin.
> Yet he does not leave the guilty unpunished;
> he punishes the children and their children
> for the sin of the parents to the third and
> fourth generation.
> Exodus 34:6b-7 (NIV)

God is loving *and* just at the same time. He is gracious *and* blameless. I began to approach Him with more humility, looking for this perfectly-balanced character of God at work in my life.

This question of God truly being enough also made me think of Abraham, the man in the Bible who waits and waits and waits for the child that God promises him. God finally proves Himself faithful with the birth of Abraham and Sarah's son, Isaac. And what happens next? God asks Abraham to sacrifice his son (Gen. 22). And Abraham faces the question, 'Is God enough?' Only in the face of God's command to sacrifice Isaac does

Abraham truly know his answer to that question. His answer is a resounding, 'Yes!' Once again, that is not the end of the story. God sends an angel to stop Abraham from following through and provides a ram to sacrifice in Isaac's place. God never asks us to give anything that He is not willing to give Himself on our behalf. He demonstrates this truth with inconceivable generosity by sending His Son, Jesus, to pay the price of death for our sins.

In light of that truth, let my answer, no matter what the circumstances, today and always be a resounding, 'Yes!' And when my heart struggles with the truth, let it be followed by, "I do believe; help me overcome my unbelief!" (Mark 9:24b NIV).

It seems like such a silly question as I write it down... of course He is enough! He is everything—the Alpha, the Omega, my Savior, Messiah, Redeemer, the One who knows me and loves me unconditionally anyway. He gave me all that I have to lose, so why shouldn't He be entitled to take it or leave it as He sees fit?

And yet, I have been struggling with this question for months. I guess you can't truly know what you can or cannot release to Him until it is time to release it, and I am tired of holding on to this one.

Father, I'm sorry for the way I've been handling the situation, looking away from you instead of running to you. After all, I am YOUR child! Do you not weep with me and bottle my tears as I grieve? I'm sorry for holding you responsible, for not giving you 'permission' to do what you will with what is yours, and for seeing myself as a victim.

Father, help free me from these thought patterns and replace the lies with truth and promises from your word.

- You have a plan for my life.
- Your plan is better than the one I have imagined for myself.
- You will use this situation for your good.
- You never leave my side, and you care for me.
- Your timing is perfect.
- Your ways are higher than my ways and your thoughts higher than my thoughts.
- You are my refuge in trouble.

I typed up this list of promises, printed it out, and kept it in my purse. I read it every day for a long, long time. I knew these things to be true in my head, but my heart was far from believing them on many days. At the end of this chapter, you will find a list of truths to read every day if you need a reminder as well. You can also use it as an outline for prayer, and there is some space to add your own reminders of God's truths that are specific to your story.

Forgive me for my frustration and my lack of faith in the last few months. Ever since the miscarriage my period has been irregular, bleeding for weeks at a time and stopping for only a week at the most before starting again. The doctor is starting me on the birth control pill for a month to help regulate my hormone levels.

This made me particularly frustrated. At the doctor's suggestion of going on birth control, I wanted to yell, 'You do realize that we are *trying* to get pregnant, right?' But surprisingly, it ended up being very helpful in getting things back on track physically.

Father, help me to be patient, to rest in you as I wait on your timing. So, I release this desire into your hands, again, as I have so many times and will continue to do. Draw me close to you!

I had grown dependent on my grief. I was afraid to begin to feel joy again because it also came with guilt that I was somehow forgetting about my baby. What a lie from Satan! Once I decided that I was ready to surrender my plans to God and trust His control, I began to experience healing.

As a person who processes my thoughts best when writing them out on paper, I had done very little of that up to this point. But once this shift in my perspective took place, I could only keep the words back for so long.

One night in August, I woke up in the middle of the night, and all of the words, which had been so jumbled up in my mind, were perfectly arranged and ready to come out. I got up, sat in the dark with my laptop, and typed up the summation of everything that I had been thinking and feeling. It was an outpouring from the heart. I wasn't sure what the purpose of recording it would be, other than to finally have some written acknowledgement of the circumstances that I was working through. I decided to post it to my blog, which up until that point had been exclusively dedicated to homesteading.

> We want to avoid suffering, death, sin, ashes. But we live in a world crushed and broken and torn, a world God Himself visited to redeem. We receive his poured-out life, and being allowed the high priviledge of suffering with Him, may then pour ourselves out for others.
>
> - *Elisabeth Elliot*

The reaction was immediate and completely unexpected—the post was shared, commented on, and reshared. Many of my acquaintances were finding out for the first time that I had even had a miscarriage. A local magazine picked it up and published it.

And then the messages started. So many women reached out to me—women who were feeling the same way, experiencing the same circumstances, struggling through the same questions. As they thanked me for sharing and expressed how much my words had helped them, I began to see the first shred of a positive outcome from the loss that I had experienced. I was humbled and overwhelmed by the outpouring of gratitude from so many mothers who were struggling in the same way.

Once I opened myself up to others, I found myself opening up more honestly with God as well. With a new humility in God's presence, I was forced to take a closer inventory of my life.

Did you know?

Pomegranates are one of the seven foods that the spies brought back from the Promised Land as an example of God's faithfulness and provision (Deut. 8:8).

The Holy Spirit began to gently point out some of the idols that I had in my life. In turning from God during my grief, I had unconsciously turned toward other things. I was not worshipping just one idol, but many: hobbies, work, family, and time-wasting activities like social media. However, the most consistent and recent idol of all was wanting to have a baby. This desire easily consumed more of my thoughts than Christ did on any given day.

The Bible makes it clear that God is a jealous God with one requirement, that He be first (Exo. 34:14). Always. Instead of seeking God for Himself, I had been seeking Him for what He could give me. To cut straight to the heart of my actions, I was trying to use Him to get a baby. When I realized this, I was ashamed! Had I truly believed that God couldn't see through my thinly-veiled attempt to get my way? I needed to straighten out my priorities if I was to be the woman that Christ desired me to be. While I did want a baby, I did not want a God who fed my self-absorption or condoned my inability to focus on His will.

While I didn't do anything to cause my miscarriage, I realized that in the way that I had responded to my loss, I did have things to be sorry for. I did have attitudes that I needed to confess. I had a responsibility to be careful to approach this issue with God's perspective and a correct view of Him. While I desperately wanted to argue that I was justified in my response as a survivor of pregnancy loss, I realized that clinging to that stance would not help me move forward. I took down the blame, doubt, guilt, shame, pride, and grief that I was working through for a moment so that I could be real and authentic with God. As I began to put God back into His proper place, it was finally time for me to confess.

Did you know?

The top of the pomegranate, or calyx, is said to be the inspiration used to design King Solomon's crown.

October 3, 2014

I am sorry that I have put other things before you, God. I confess that I have put my own will above your will at the risk of your kingdom. I am sorry that I have questioned your love, that I have been tempted to give blame to you when the true sinner is myself, and for not recognizing that the ultimate blame is on Satan for his temptation in the garden. Satan is so tricky to deceive us into blaming you for his handiwork!

    I confess that I have wanted my great faith and my own dreams to be an answer and solution to the problem, instead of having faith in you and your will, that you are working all things together for good. I humble myself and submit to your will.

    Forgive me. Give me patience. Give me strength. Give me a renewed mind and spirit. But above all else, give me a desire for you first and foremost. For you are making all things new!

My flawed perspective gave way to renewed faith. At least, for a while.

When Experiencing HONESTY

When you finally come to the place where you are ready to face the deep questions lurking in the dark places of your heart and mind, that is a great sign! It is time to look for answers! As much as possible, put aside the hurt, blame, guilt, and all of the rest of those emotions and truly seek God's wisdom in the Bible.

Those who finally come to the end of themselves, turn to God's wisdom, and surrender honestly and vulnerably to Him will find truth, healing, and redemption. Only when we finally get to the point of being truly honest with ourselves and God can He begin to redeem what was lost. He can reveal Himself and demonstrate His character in our lives.

You may have had some of the same questions that I did, but you may have many more as well, depending on your circumstances. Use the space provided at the end of this chapter to write out your questions and any scripture references and answers that you discover.

God is not afraid of your questions. He is the Beginning and the End, and He is more than capable of satisfying your longing for understanding. But let me also interject a quick disclaimer—just because God is capable of answering, doesn't mean that He is required to grant answers how and when we demand them. Demanding answers is not going to result in much revelation, I'm afraid. However, remember that verse about God having good plans for us? Let's read it in context and see one of God's most comforting promises.

This is what the Lord says: "When seventy years are completed for Babylon, I will come to you and fulfill my good promise to bring you back to this place. For I know the plans I have for you," declares the Lord, "plans to prosper you and not to harm you, plans to give you hope and a future. Then you will call on me and come and pray to me, and I will listen to you. You will seek me and find me when you seek me with all your heart. I will be found by you," declares the Lord, "and will bring you back from captivity. I will gather you from all the nations and places where I have banished you," declares the Lord, "and will bring you back to the place from which I carried you into exile."

Jeremiah 29:10-14 (NIV)

  The promise is that when you seek God with your whole heart, honestly desiring to know Him and His will, then you will find the answer that satisfies your soul. Spoiler alert—He is the answer! In our process of searching for answers, we will find Him! He is not trying to hide from us. He wants us to find Him! He wants us to see our pain from His eternal perspective. He wants us to rest in His peace, which is beyond our earthly understanding. He wants us to be flooded by assurance of His great love. This is the part where we begin to fall in love with Him all over again! He has been waiting expectantly for this moment.

Think about Job, who continually asks God His questions with honesty throughout his grief and loss. When God finally shows up with a reply, it isn't to explain Himself or provide the reasoning behind the circumstances. It is to declare His sovereignty and character (Job 38-41). He doesn't give an answer; He is the answer.

You see, tragedy and triumph go together. When we overcome pain with the love of Christ, when we embrace grief, knowing that God will lead us through the valley of the shadow of death to the other side (Ps. 23:4), there is a promise for those who are faithful. This promise is not that our dreams will come true, as we so often want to believe, and it is not that we will get our way. It is that we will know God, that His will be done in us, and that He be glorified.

❦ When NOT Experiencing HONESTY ❦

Everyone moves through the grief process at their own pace. Each person is picking up this book and reading it from a unique place in their journey through grief. The timeline is different for everyone, and I encourage you to take your time working through the different seasons. Rushing through the process will hinder its completion.

If you are reading and realize that you are not at the honest stage yet, and you are still experiencing emotional instability, then don't feel pressured to read any further in the book until you are ready. It took me a long time to reach the point of honesty, but I was not open to what God had to say to me until I made that shift in my perspective. I do not want you to read the following sections and hear a message of guilt, shame, or condemnation, but rather one of life, hope, and redemption.

Let me also say that there wasn't a specific day when I suddenly moved out of emotional instability and entered honesty. It was a constant back and forth, day-by-day struggle (as you will see in the next chapter). If you aren't ready to brooch honesty at all yet, there is no shame in that. Come back when you are. I'll wait right here for you, no matter how long it takes.

Truth to Read Everyday

God is with me (Is. 41:10)
- The Holy Spirit dwells inside of me (John 14:16)
- God is present in my pain (Is. 57:15)

God holds time in His hands (Ecc. 3:11)
- He knows the correct time of all things. (Ps. 31:15)
- He knows if and when I will have children. (Jer. 29:11)

God created me in His image (Gen. 1:27)
- He knows my body, and He is not limited by any problems that I have. (Matt. 10:30)
- I am not broken—I am fearfully and wonderfully made. (Ps. 139:14)

God has a good and perfect plan for me (Rom. 12:2)
- I am where I am right now for a reason. (Ecc. 3:1-8)
- He has created me for the purpose of glorifying Him. (1 Chron. 16:9-10)

God shares in my pain. (Ps. 147:3)
- He loves me so much that He sacrificed His child for me. (John 3:16)
- He mourns with me and bottles up my tears. (Ps. 56:8)

God has blessed me incredibly (James 1:17)
- I can focus on what I do have rather than what I do not. (1 Thess. 5:18)

God can use this loss for good. (Gen. 50:20)
- He will use even this loss to display His glory in time. (John 9:3)

God is in the work of restoration. (Is. 43:19)
- He is redeeming every loss and making all things new. (Rev. 21:5)

My Questions and God's Answers

My Questions and God's Answers

My Questions and God's Answers

My Questions and God's Answers

SIX

IMPATIENCE

*"How long, O LORD?
Will You forget me forever?
How long will You hide Your face from me?
How long must I wrestle with my thoughts,
and day after day have sorrow in my heart?"*

— *Psalm 13:1–2a (NIV)*

Wow! God was teaching me so many things! Surely, with this new biblical perspective, I would be able to free myself from all of the emotional entanglements of the miscarriage, right? I can scripturally rationalize my way out of grief! Wrong. Grieving is a process. Two steps forward, one step back.

At the beginning of October, I participated in a walk in honor of lost babies. A friend from church, who had dealt with infertility for years before adopting one child and then having two more children, heard about the event and offered to go with me. I wasn't really sure what to expect, but I decided to sign up and go.

I went by myself, planning to meet my friend there. I was an emotional wreck (yes, still). The sorrow seemed to come in waves. I would do well for a while, and then something, even the smallest thing, would cause the pain and emotion to resurface. This was one of those days.

I got to the event, surprised to see that the park was filled with families. I hadn't realized that it was a family event. Suddenly, I desperately wanted Nathan to be there with me and felt very alone. I remember sitting on the edge of a fountain in the middle of the park on the verge of tears.

Even when surrounded by women who knew my pain, I felt like every person there could see straight through me and into my empty womb. I wanted to melt into the ground. I wanted to have someone wrap me in their arms and hold together all of the broken pieces. I didn't want to have a reason to be there.

I want you to remember this spot at the fountain, because this is not the last time that I will be sitting there. Our God is the Redeemer, and He saw me sitting at the fountain that day. And He was already planning to redeem this moment years later.

The event was really well done. The organizers gathered everyone together and read the names of all of the babies represented that day and dates of loss, including 'Baby Greneaux.' Then each person received a balloon to represent their child and took a silent walk around the lake before everyone released the balloons together.

Hearing all of the names read aloud made me feel grateful. Many of the children had names, which meant they were lost much later in pregnancy than mine, after the gender could be known. Some had birthdays, which meant that they had died as infants or hours after a premature birth. Some families had experienced multiple losses. It was also encouraging that many of the families had children with them—a sign of hope for those of us still without.

Later in October, Nathan and I took the trip to China that we had booked the day of the devastating ultrasound. I couldn't help but be a little disappointed that I still wasn't pregnant, and the trip, which I thought would surely be interrupted by the conception of a new baby, was happening uninhibited. On the other hand, I'm so glad we took that trip. It was an incredible experience to see so much of China with my husband, and for the first time in a long time, I began to feel a little lighter.

More time passed, and before I knew it, our baby's would-be due date was around the corner.

December 5, 2014

I took down the crib today. Yes, it has been up this whole time as a symbol of hope and faith that getting pregnant again was just a day away. But it is time to accept reality. As the would-be due date approaches, I know it is time to accept the truth. I am not pregnant, and it could be a long time before it happens. However, if I was supposed to have a baby right now, then I would, so obviously God has me right where He wants me at this time. And I am learning to rest in that truth.

When the due date came and went, Nathan suggested that we book another trip, this time to Ireland in May. In the months that followed, we continued trying to have a baby. This season was torture. Every month I would get my hopes up only to be let down over and over again. I began to wonder if we would ever get pregnant again. Friends who had gotten pregnant after I had the miscarriage now had babies in their arms, but I still wasn't expecting. While I had finally dealt with the loss related to the miscarriage, I was now dealing with the grief of waiting for another chance to try again.

I thought that I had come so far! I had grown spiritually by leaps and bounds. My emotional health was definitely improved. I thought the growth I had experienced would help me learn to cope in a healthier way. Many times it did, but that wasn't always the case.

I still struggled with babies in general. Babies are sweet and adorable, and I wanted one more than anything, but they sure could make me angry! It wouldn't be every day, but some days, I really disliked everyone who had a baby. I would get overly annoyed when someone complained about their kids. Or said that I was lucky not to have any. Or got pregnant without trying. Or...well, you get the idea. No one did these things to intentionally upset me, but it was a challenge to not take everything personally.

Some days I would wake up, and everything seemed great. I had a purpose. If I never had a baby, I knew that it would be just fine. I could have weeks of these good days, or even months.

But sooner or later, I would wake up one day, and it was not okay. I had waited and waited. I was doing everything right. Life was not fair. I would get discouraged. My friend's baby born long after I started trying was celebrating their first birthday, or second. I couldn't make it one more day like this! Something had to give!

Something did give. Thankfully, what gave was my selfish attitude. After some bad days, I would wake up one morning and realize that it was another good day, and I was okay with life just the way things were. It probably would have helped my husband if there were some kind of meter to show him which day I was on, but I tried to keep him up to date as much as possible!

While I had been experiencing a lack of motivation during the depression phase of grief, I was now recovering my usual goal-oriented attitude. And what better goal than to figure out how to have a baby? If there was a way for me to solve the pregnancy problem through logic, research, science, or simple creativity, I was going to find it!

As the months of unfulfilled waiting continued, I grew impatient with God's timing. It was so tempting to pick up the phone or computer, determined to find the answers, seeking the right diet, exercise, or piece of advice that would solve all my problems. A persistent and independent character had served me well in many areas of life. However, using it to force my will and demand answers in this season did not. Grief was not a problem for me to fix and overcome; it was a season that God was using to shape and mold me to become more like Christ. After all, who experienced grief to the fullest more than our Savior Himself?

It brings to mind the story of the potter and the clay in Jeremiah 18 in which God, depicted as a potter, exerts his right to create the clay into whatever object and purpose He sees fit. There is only one way for a good creation to be molded into a better one. It must be completely destroyed into a shapeless lump of clay, violently thrown onto the wheel once again, and then carefully shaped into the beautiful masterpiece that the artist has in mind. The process in my own life was painful, and it was difficult not to focus on the loss, because I couldn't see the end result that God had in mind. But the transformation process of grief was the only way I could become who God intended me to be.

I was so much like Abraham in the Old Testament. God promises him countless descendants, but when the fulfillment of that promise seems impossible, Abraham takes matters into his own hands. He sleeps with his servant and has a child through her in an attempt to carry on his family line (Gen. 16). Taking the initiative seems like a positive character trait, unless it is used to force our version of what we think God's will should be, rather than waiting on His timing. If I could have done anything to get my way, I would have given it a try.

Did you know?

The tops of the columns in Solomon's temple were engraved with images of pomegranates.

I started keeping careful notes about my cycles in my calendar. There is a great deal to keep track of if you are charting cycles. I created my own system of keeping up with all the symptoms: circles meant one thing, squares another, and lines another, not to mention diagrams and numbers. It was starting to look like a Pollock painting!

If I was unable to sleep in the middle of the night, I would scroll through 'trying to conceive' forums for hours, scouring for any tips or information that might be able to unlock my fertility potential. I quickly learned an entirely new language comprised of so many acronyms it made my head spin! Anyone TTC using OPKs to detect O will debate on using FMU or how many DPOs to wait before using an HPT until AF visits. If you aren't sure what any of that means, don't worry, you aren't missing out. Not surprisingly, reading forums did not get me pregnant. Besides, most of the comments were TMI.

When none of my efforts resulted in a positive pregnancy test, I had to learn how to cope with the waiting. I had to fill the time with something. Meanwhile, everyone kept telling me that once I stopped thinking about it, I would get pregnant. First of all, that logic makes no sense. Secondly, getting pregnant was absolutely all I could think about, so that wasn't really an option. At the same time, I knew that if I couldn't intentionally turn my thoughts to other pursuits, I would drive myself crazy. I took some very purposeful steps to guard my fragile heart, mind, and my soul in this season of waiting.

I started by strictly limiting my social media intake. Facebook was not my friend. All those baby pictures, baby bumps, and pregnancy announcements did not foster a positive outlook at all. I had to resist the urge to add baby stuff to my secret Pinterest board. Pinning articles about making my own baby food and that super cute, gender-neutral nursery color palette would only make me envy what others had.

And Google. I had to force myself to quit Googling. While I knew that there was no secret position, food, vitamin, supplement, phase of the moon, etc. that would magically get me pregnant, it was so tempting to look anyway. Most forums offered false hope with strange, one-in-a-million scenarios that I'm sure weren't even true. I had to fight the constant urge to research and find the answer that would make all of my pregnancy dreams come true.

Let's stop for just a moment and explore that urge, because it is good for me to be informed, right? Well, it depends on my motivation. Information is good, but when I was being honest with myself, I realized that what I was really doing was trying to force my will again. Was God capable of giving me a baby no matter what the circumstances? Yes. Everything is possible with God (Matt. 19:26). So, if I really believed that, would I be obsessively searching for a quick fix, rather than waiting on His timing? No.

I had to stop the internal debates. You know which ones I'm talking about. Every little change in my body from month to month seemed to be a sign. Going to the bathroom in the middle of the night, my skin breaking out, or feeling moody could mean that I was pregnant! But I tried not to think about it, because I didn't want to get myself too excited just to let myself down. Again. But then again, all the signs were looking up this time. This could be the month! But what if it really was nothing? There was no use in thinking about it for another two weeks until I could take the pregnancy test. Two weeks! Torture! Stop. The. Madness. Knowing whether or not I was pregnant the moment that it happened would not change the facts, so I had to intentionally turn my focus to other things and be patient. Ugh.

All of my emotions in the waiting period seemed to cycle with my body every twenty-eight days—anxiety, hope, waiting, and disappointment continually on repeat. Month after month. Another failure. Another negative pregnancy test. It was easy to fall apart every month with the disappointment. I finally decided to use something other than the month to keep track of the time. I would wait until I got to the bottom of a bottle of prenatal vitamins. I could hold it together for one hundred days until I took that last pill, and then have a day where I would fall apart. It was really just a mind game, but finding something longer term to use as a timekeeper really helped me have a more positive outlook during the waiting.

  I am a planner, which means I usually have all kinds of projects lined up. When I was trying to conceive, it was difficult not to base all decisions about future plans around possible due dates. The thought process would go something like this: 'Do I want to teach a dance class? Well, if I get pregnant tomorrow, then I will be 4 months pregnant at the end. Can I teach dance while being 4 months pregnant?' There are so many things that I said 'yes' to during my season of waiting that my "hopeful calendar" would have told me to turn down. I am so glad that I did not miss out on those experiences. My husband constantly encouraged me to create plans, take trips, and make commitments.

  Keeping busy also helped me keep my mind off of what I was missing. Staying present in my childless circumstances was difficult. I wanted a baby! I wanted the baby shower, the cute nursery, and the life of being a mommy. But that was not my life at the time. I had to fight the urge to peruse the baby aisle at Target or buy that really cute preggo shirt that was on clearance. There could be a day and time for all of that, but it was not that day. That day I was child-free. So I had to go do something that could only be done that day. I tried to focus on what was happening around me then and there, and let the future take care of itself.

In my experience, the most difficult part of the waiting period was simply not knowing how long it would last. If I knew that it would be one year, or ten years, then I could wait patiently, knowing that there was an end in sight. Even if we would never have a baby, knowing that much would have been helpful, because we would have known to move on with our lives. But waiting with an uncertain future made the delay seem unbearable.

I began to experience something of an identity crisis. What am I here for? What is the best way to use my time while waiting? Is there a reason I don't have kids yet? Is there something that I am supposed to do first? Is there already a kid out there for me that I'm supposed to adopt? Is there something wrong with me? Am I broken? Am I inadequate? Am I not supposed to have kids? Or is it all just without purpose and the way things are? Am I okay with the possibility of never being a mom? How much longer will or should I wait? Is there some lesson that I am supposed to be learning in this season? If so, can I just learn it already so that I can move on? I didn't have the answers. All I had were questions. Lots of questions.

I started my search for answers by Googling. You would think that I would know better by now! But no. I learn the hard way. When I Googled 'Bible verses about infertility and miscarriage,' I got two pages of flowery promises that "in all things God works for the good of those who love him" (Rom. 8:28 NIV), and "about this time next year...you will hold a son in your arms" (2 Kings 4:16 NIV), and "I will surely bless you and make your descendants as numerous as the stars in the sky" (Gen. 22:17 NIV). If these verses were meant to comfort me as a hurting woman, they failed miserably. They only made me question more why these promises weren't coming true in my own life.

> "Biblically, waiting is not just something we have to do until we get what we want. Waiting is part of the process of becoming what God wants us to be."
> - John Ortberg

I wanted desperately to grab hold of these prophesies and wrap them around me like a warm, fuzzy blanket and pretend that they were meant for me. I wanted to take the promise that God gives to Hannah, who gives birth to Samuel after years of infertility, and claim it as my own (1 Sam. 1). But I didn't want to have to turn around and give my long-awaited child back to God, as Hannah does. I wanted to take the covenant that God makes with Abraham and Sarah to give them countless descendants and pretend that it was a covenant with me (Gen. 15-21). But I didn't want to wait until I was ninety years old to finally give birth, as Sarah does. I wanted to give birth to children who grew into great men and women of faith, as Rachel did with Joseph (Gen. 30). But I didn't want to have to watch the women around me give birth to child after child while I pleaded with God for a son, as Rachel does.

I wanted God to write the same story in my life that he had written in so many other women's lives throughout the Bible. I clung to these redemptive stories and wanted the happy endings, but I glossed over the years of struggle, pain, confusion, and fruitless faith that these women endured before seeing their promises from God fulfilled.

I eventually had to face the honest truth that God had given me no such promise. No angel had announced to me that I would have a child. No prophet had told me that I would hold a son in my arms in one year's time. I had no covenant with God that countless descendants were in my future. I had to accept that I wasn't meant to know the answers, nor could I handle all of the answers. Some things in God's plan will always remain mysterious because, well, He is God. I had to come to terms with the fact that God was writing a unique story just for me. It would look different from anything that He had ever done before or would ever do again.

So if the promises to those women in the Bible are not meant for us, why do we have all of these stories? Why do we get to hear all of the ways that God works in other people's lives, if we can't claim those same results in our own? While scouring these stories for consolation, I discovered that while the specific promises may not be the same, the God who makes them is.

In each story, I discovered a new piece of God's character. While His plans for each of our lives are different, His character is unchanging. In Sarah's story, He is the God who keeps His promises. In Hannah's, He is gracious. In Rachel's, He is sovereign. I stopped grabbing hold of these examples, showing them to God, and expecting to get my way. Instead, I started to fall in love with the God who I witnessed carefully weaving redemption into story after story. I stopped skipping ahead to the endings and watched God comfort, grow, and guide these women in their doubt, confusion, impatience, and frustration.

I got to see behind the scenes how God was putting into motion a good plan in each of their lives, even when they couldn't see it. I got to witness how God works outside of the linear time constraints that confine our perspectives. I got to see their entire story, already redeemed and complete, just as God does. Was it truly possible that the God who wrote these incredible stories, was also writing mine?

As I took in the entire scope of the narrative, I realized something profound: finally having a child is not what makes these women's lives more fulfilling or allows God's redemption to take place. Restoration is made possible through their faith; through the process of releasing their hopes and dreams to the Lord in order for Him to do His will, no matter what the end result. It was letting God's will be displayed in them, at the expense of their own desires. Slowly, I began to believe that I could also trust God with my life and my desires.

When Experiencing IMPATIENCE

It was easy to get discouraged when I looked at everyone with babies and me without one. However, if I made a list of all of the amazing things that I had been blessed with while being completely undeserving, I could fill a book. Instead of putting my attention on what I didn't have, I had to make an intentional effort to be thankful for the many blessings in life that I did have! You can use the space provided at the end of this chapter to create your own gratitude list. I highly recommend doing this to help keep your waiting in perspective.

Whatever kind of day you are having, and no matter how long you wait, know that God's timing is perfect. And more importantly, know that God has not forgotten you. When you remain in the present moment, you are right in the center of His will. Keep your eyes on Him—there is a lot to be learned in the waiting. Who you are and who you become in this season of faith not-yet-fulfilled is the truest reflection of your character. Make it beautiful, rather than bitter!

Gratitude for Blessings

Gratitude for Blessings

SEVEN

SUBMISSION

*"Though the fig tree does not bud
and there are no grapes on the vines,
though the olive crop fails
and the fields produce no food,
though there are no sheep in the pen
and no cattle in the stalls,
yet I will rejoice in the Lord,
I will be joyful in God my Savior.
The Sovereign Lord is my strength;
He makes my feet like the feet of a deer,
He enables me to tread on the heights."*

Habakkuk 3:17-19 (NIV)

Slowly, God changed the way that I viewed everything—my definition of family, what my future could hold, and how to depend on Him in the midst of uncertainty.

> "There's some task which the God of all the universe, the great Creator, your redeemer in Jesus Christ has for you to do, and which will remain undone and incomplete until by faith and obedience you step into the will of God."
> - Alan Redpath

I had to look at my situation with faith, but not a faith that believed that my will should come to pass. I needed a faith that trusted that God's will for me was ultimately greater for His glory. Only then could I receive His peace and have the opportunity to joyfully take part in what He was doing. In this life, we are not promised health and wealth, but we are guaranteed hardship and sacrifice (John 16:33). God will use every detail of our story, even the consequences of sin, to work together for the good of those who love Him (Rom. 8:28), even though that good may not take the form we expect it to.

August 4, 2015

I can't believe it has been eight months since I have touched this journal. It isn't that I haven't thought about it—our family situation is almost all I think about—I am just never sure what to say. Here is a quick update on what has happened. The doctor said there was no reason to start any testing until August (now) but this past March, I took an ovulation predictor kit that came back positive twelve days in a row.

    Yeah, that isn't normal. My doctor is very laid back and said that we should wait a full year of trying after my cycle returned to normal before starting any kind of fertility testing. But when I got these ovulation test results, I called him to let him know. He agreed that there must be something not quite right and encouraged me to begin some blood work to find the issue.
    In April, I had a particularly difficult month. It was time for my birthday again, but all I could think about was the joy that I had experienced the year before. I had been filled with so much hope and happiness. I told Nathan that I didn't want to celebrate my birthday at all because I couldn't stop the memories from flooding back, not to mention my discouragement that after a full year, we were still stuck in the same circumstances. I thought that surely a year later we wouldn't still be trying to get pregnant again. My birthday passed without celebration.

    So they tested my blood and found out that I wasn't ovulating, which is the technical definition of infertility.

    I got these test results the week of Mother's Day.

Oh, Mother's Day. How I resent you. So on Mother's Day 2015, I was getting used to the idea that I was infertile. For the first time, I began to seriously consider the possibility of us not ever being able to conceive. Hearing this news in such an official way felt, in some ways, like a death sentence. Not a literal death, but the death of the dream that I had always had of what my family would look like. It was, once again, devastating.

It took me a while to get used to the idea. I was frustrated that we had wasted so much time but glad that this turn of events had started the process of finding out what is wrong. More tests showed good hormone levels, but crazy hypothyroidism, so they sent me to an endocrinologist.

I have to add in some details about this process, because God is so good! All of this blood work has to be done on specific days of the cycle to get the correct results. Remember that trip to Ireland that we had planned? Well, the right day for my testing was the day after we would be getting back in the country from our trip.

On our way home, we got stuck in the Houston airport during a huge thunderstorm. Our flight was delayed and eventually canceled. We slept on the airport floor that night while on standby for any outgoing flights. The entire time we were stuck, I was so stressed out that we wouldn't get home in time to do the blood work, and we would have to wait another month to do it. Another month! Why is it always one more month? I was so frustrated with God. Just when it seemed like we would be finding some answers, He had me back in a place of feeling stuck (quite literally).

We got a flight out early the following morning, and when we landed at home, we drove directly from the airport to the lab to do the bloodwork. We had hardly slept, were completely stressed out, and ravenously hungry. We were looking rough! But it's a good thing we made it: the results showed that my thyroid levels were completely off. I was glad to know that we had at least found something wrong, because then we knew what needed to be fixed.

Two weeks later at the endocrinologist, they ran the same blood work as before, with a few additional tests. Surprisingly, my initial thyroid levels came back within a normal range, but the more extensive testing showed some serious problems. The doctor explained that I had Hashimoto's disease. With this disease, the thyroid levels are strongly affected by anxiety. Since I was completely stressed when I had taken the testing the first time around, it raised the red flag that I needed more in-depth testing.

If we hadn't been stuck in the Houston airport overnight, the odds were that my thyroid levels would have looked fine on the surface, and they wouldn't have tested further to discover the problem. Have you ever been mad at God about something and then realized how completely loving He was being in the act that you were so upset about? Yeah, that was me.

There they discovered in June that I have Hashimoto's disease, an autoimmune disorder where antibodies attack my thyroid, causing hypothyroidism.

There is a long list of symptoms of Hashimoto's, but the only one that I was really concerned with was increased rates of miscarriage and infertility. The disease is closely linked with reproductive health, and the severity of the disease usually increases with each pregnancy. If this truly was the cause of our pregnancy troubles, then we may have been on our way to finding a solution. But there was also a high likelihood that if we could get pregnant, we may experience another miscarriage, unless my thyroid levels were closely monitored and regulated.

So now I am taking thyroid medicine every day for the rest of my life and am gluten free. I'm glad we caught it early but am not enjoying being a 'high-maintenance' eater. It isn't much of a sacrifice if it means I can get pregnant.

We learned that gluten could aggravate the symptoms of Hashimoto's, and that information resulted in a quick diet change. I love my gluten! But, at that point, if someone had told me that standing on my head would get me pregnant, I would have done it! So yeah, gluten was easy to give up in the situation. Totally worth it. I was not a huge fan of the idea of being on medication for the rest of my life, either, but once again, whatever would work was fine with me.

But we don't really know if this is even related, so we are scheduled to see a fertility specialist later this week. While a lot of time is passing in this process, I have started counting how much time I have SAVED, and God has continued to show me His faithfulness. Here are just a few ways:

- The crazy results from the ovulation kit allowed us to start testing in March instead of waiting until August.
- My hormone blood work had to be done on day three of my cycle, which was going to be during our Ireland trip, and I would have to wait another month, but I started late and was able to take the test the day we got home (the timing of which still worked out perfectly, even being stranded in the airport an extra day).
- My thyroid levels in that test were WAY off, but just two weeks later they were normal—if that hadn't been the case, we never would have discovered the Hashimoto's.
- When I scheduled my endocrinologist appointment, it was a two month wait, but they called back an hour later with an opening the next day! Not to mention that was the only day all summer that I

would be able to get away from the kids at work for a little while to go!

These are not coincidences. God's timing is perfect. He could have made these events come to pass at any time. He was in control of the speed at which everything began to fall into place.

God is good. He does have a plan, and I can see that in so many little ways.

What I share next is truly an example of how God had been slowly changing my idea of what our family could look like. For the first time, I had become open to whatever He may have for me, rather than digging in my heels and clinging to what I had originally wanted for Nathan and myself.

Other than just doctors' appointments, we have been pursuing something else as well. I don't know when the idea first started, but we began seriously contemplating adoption in May. We both feel that there are lots of kids in the U.S. that need adoption, and among those, we are most interested in foster-to-adoption through the state.

This is so different from what I would have told you a year ago, but I am slowly breaking down all of the barriers of what I 'won't' do. Maybe it is my work at Bridge that has given me a desire to help kids in desperate situations or even given me the idea that I may have the ability to help them at all.

I have gone from thinking that fostering is too hard, to saying only an infant that doesn't have too much baggage, to any young (elementary and under) age, but only one child to start off with. Who knows where we will end up at this rate? We went to the orientation and are trying to decide which dates to start the classes. My biggest concerns going into this are:

Will it hurt my relationship with Nathan?

Adding any new person into the family mix, even a baby of our own, will cause tension and strain because it is a huge adjustment. I just want to make sure that I can put Nathan over any kids and keep open and honest communication as we go through all of the decisions involved.

What to do about my job?

If we were adopting, then I would quit to be a stay-at-home mom, but with fostering, there is no guarantee how long they will be with you. It could be two weeks or forever! So do I put them in daycare? The logistics on this one really have me stumped. But I know it's no big thing for God.

How will our families react?

I honestly have no idea what they will say...

At this point I can't say that God has called us to

do this. He has been pretty silent through most of this process. I would love to say that I have prayed about it a lot, but that isn't true either. In all honesty, I think that in some ways I am still having trouble trusting God. I don't doubt His goodness or sovereignty, which is why I can't trust Him.

Even after all of this time, I was still having trouble trusting God, because I couldn't trust Him to do what I wanted Him to do. If He had allowed a miscarriage to happen in the past, there was nothing to keep Him from allowing another miscarriage to happen in the future. And yet, submission to His will and ultimately trusting that His way was best was the only way forward.

There is no guarantee that children are His plan for us—I know that if I do get pregnant again, I will be terrified about having another miscarriage. He is going to do His will, and while I know His will is best, I also know it is quite different from any family picture I had in mind.

Father, whatever you have in store for me, I pray that you would help me to follow and accept it with joy. While the last twenty months have been such a long journey, I have a feeling this is only the beginning. Father, would you give me clarity? Would you show me the direction we should take with upcoming decisions?

In the past you have shown me your will so clearly,

and I pray that you would do that for Nathan and me in this situation. I especially pray that you would give Nathan confidence in your calling and allow him to lead in this. Whatever happens, we know that you are sovereign, and we are only here to do your will and bring you glory!

    I just want to say that while I had prayed and asked God for clarity many times, this was the first time I finally put it on paper. There is something very permanent about writing something down. It can't be erased or unwritten. I can't go back and edit my journal to show that God answered a prayer in a way that He really didn't. I can't take away the doubts and questions that I was experiencing.

    That permanence in writing down prayers and thoughts is what makes seeing God's answers later so amazing. For me, this was absolutely the case with the journal entry above. In the next chapter, you will see what God already knew when I was writing these very words. Was it a coincidence that I was just then pouring out my heart in this journal after eight months of silence? Absolutely not. God has such an incredible way of making Himself known in the most intimate moments with undeniable certainty. I was asking for clarity, and He was about to give it to me.

⁕ When Experiencing SUBMISSION ⁕

In the grief process the word "acceptance" usually refers to coming to terms with what happened. However, I find the term "submission" more accurate in describing the necessary step to proceed as Christians. Submission in this instance describes coming to terms with who God truly is and finally reaching a point of surrendering to His will. It is acknowledging that we must release what we think we are entitled to in order to see the fulfillment of His will for us. When we truly live in submission, we give God the key to unlock the floodgates of redemption in our lives.

There is space on the following page to journal about some areas that you recognize as needing submission in your own life. Use this space to make a list, write out a prayer of submission to God, or write your thoughts about any ideas, dreams, expectations, or entitlements that you are still holding on to. Try to include some steps of how you can submit that area in a practical way.

What I Need to Submit

What I Need to Submit

EIGHT

FEAR

"'About this time next year,' Elisha said, 'you will hold a son in your arms.'

'No, my lord!' she objected. 'Please, man of God, don't mislead your servant!'"

— 2 Kings 4:16 (NIV)

My previous journal entry was on August fourth. I had asked God for clarity. I had surrendered my will to His. I had come to a place of accepting whatever His future for me might hold. Three weeks later, my journal continues.

August 30, 2015

Yes, I am just now writing this after getting the news two and a half weeks ago—we are pregnant! What a crazy month it has been. We went to see the specialist on the tenth, and he scheduled lots of tests to be started on day three of my cycle. The only problem was that I was two weeks late and not showing signs of starting any time soon.

I finally wondered if I could be pregnant—the idea popped into my head at ten o'clock on a Tuesday night. I mentioned it to Nathan, and he suggested we go get a test right then, so we went to the 24 hour CVS. Of course, I wanted to save money, so I opted for the line version rather than the digital, went home, took the test, and it showed that I was pregnant.

In complete denial, we decided it couldn't be true, and we needed the digital test. I drank a bunch of water, we went back to CVS, got the digital test, waited an hour, and took it. Pregnant!

After waiting for this moment for so long, I thought I would be jumping up and down, shouting the news at the top of my lungs, but instead Nathan and I just sat there staring at it for half an hour in disbelief. I didn't realize how strong of a protective wall I had built around my heart until that moment. I think it will take a long time before I am excited about this pregnancy.

I'm happy, but not the same carefree giddiness that I had the first time.

I was completely surprised by my reaction. I knew that God would not give me anything that I could not overcome with His help and His strength carrying me through it. But deep inside, I was afraid that I wouldn't be able to deal with another miscarriage. I was afraid of losing myself again.

I'm pretty sure Nathan was, too. He had so patiently walked beside me through my grief, even when he couldn't understand what I was experiencing. It is incredibly difficult to watch someone that you love walk through a painful season and feel powerless to help them. I knew that the grief process had been just as hard on him as it had been on me, although in a completely different way.

That night, I kept asking Nathan, "Do you really think I'm pregnant?" Of course, we both knew the answer was yes, what I really wanted to know was, 'Do you think I'll really have a baby?' The answer to that has yet to be seen, and only time will tell.

I had been wanting to know the end of my story for so long, anticipating whatever came next, and hating being stuck. For the first time, I wasn't sure that I wanted to know the ending. I wasn't sure it would be a happy culmination, and I didn't dare allow myself to hope for one! There was another question lurking in the back of my mind that I didn't want to ask, because I didn't want to know the answer—if God wants me to surrender everything to Him, what else will He ask me to give? And will I be willing to do so? I had been able to submit when I had nothing left, but now that I once again had something to lose, I wasn't so sure.

Only four days after the appointment at the fertility specialist, we called back to say we were pregnant. He only sees patients pre-pregnancy unless they have already had an appointment, so we will do all of our early pregnancy visits through them—another of God's mercies.

This was definitely an incredible gift from God, because it meant that our first ultrasound would be done in the office at the fertility clinic, rather than my regular doctor's office. I honestly don't think I would have been able to walk into the same room, where I had received such devastating news, without having an emotional breakdown.

Within the first week of finding out, they put me on progesterone and did two sets of blood work to make sure everything was progressing correctly.

The staff members at the fertility clinic were amazing! They were sensitive to my fragile feelings and took every precaution to make sure that we did everything possible to keep the baby healthy and safe. We scheduled thyroid appointments with the endocrinologist every six weeks to check blood work and regulate my medicine accordingly throughout the entire pregnancy.

On August twenty-first we had our first ultrasound. The week leading up to this was rough. I would play out in my head the worst scenarios possible and felt like I was reliving that day in the ultrasound room all over again. I would cry as if I had lost the baby, even though all of our tests have come back looking good. I was eager for, and equally afraid of, what I would see in the ultrasound.

But God's grace was overflowing the day of the test, and I was completely filled with peace! It was still very early, but we got to see our baby. They think we were about six weeks at that point, but too early for a due date. And then, we got to hear the heartbeat! What a beautiful little sound! And I cried tears of relief. We have another ultrasound scheduled for this

Friday to check the growth rate. If all is well at that point, we will be further along than last time. For now, I am taking things one day at a time and trying to be thankful for the time that we have with this baby, whether it be a few weeks or for the rest of our lives.

We have only told my parents so far. I want to wait until I can genuinely share in the joy of the moment. I am struggling with a lot of fatigue and a little morning sickness, but I keep reminding myself to be grateful for it as a healthy sign.

Father, thank you for this undeserved gift! I pray that you would continue to give me peace over the next few months, and that I would have the strength to thank you and give you glory no matter what the outcome. I give this child to you, because I know that you love it, and have created it for a good purpose—giving you glory.

I pray that with time you would increase my joy—that my past grief wouldn't steal the happiness that comes with welcoming and celebrating a new life. I love you and thank you for your faithfulness and sovereignty. I trust you completely with all I have.

This is where my pregnancy journal ends.

What? Why? We were just getting to the good part, right? I stopped journaling, because I was too afraid to write anything down. Through the miscarriage and infertility, I wrote down my thoughts and feelings, even if it was sporadic. But now that I was pregnant again, I couldn't seem to put pen to paper. I remember very distinctly what I was feeling in this season, though.

GUILT

The first emotion that dominated this season was guilt. Yes, guilt, and on so many levels! I felt guilty for not feeling the excitement that I had expected to feel. Why wasn't I overjoyed about being pregnant? Wasn't this the greatest gift that we had been waiting and praying for for so long? Shouldn't I have been blissfully happy, instead of full of fear, doubt, and dread?

I also felt guilty that I was pregnant. So many other women had expressed their similar struggles during this time of loss and waiting, and we shared a kindred bond in that season. But for all of the times that I had looked at other pregnant women and asked in envy, "God, why them and not me?" I was now asking myself the exact opposite in humility, "God, why me and not them?"

I have so many precious friends, who are still waiting even as I write these words. There is nothing that sets me apart as deserving a child any more or less than them. My faith is not greater. God does not love me more. There is no distinction. God is simply writing a different story of redemption in their lives than He is in mine. I was afraid to share my news with these friends because I knew all too well how they would feel as a result of being left behind once again. I also feared that they would not understand my reluctance to rejoice in the pregnancy.

FEAR

The main feeling that dominated, though, was fear. I have never been a fearful person, but I was suddenly paralyzed with fear. I was afraid that we would lose the baby again. I was afraid that I wouldn't be strong enough to walk through that season of loss again. I was afraid that the trust that I was finally able to place in God would be shattered all over again. I was afraid that God's promise to carry me through the difficult times in life wouldn't be enough, even though He had just proven Himself faithful to me! I was afraid that I would fall back into the dark hole that I had finally emerged from and lose myself again.

> "No one ever told me that grief felt so much like fear."
> - C. S. Lewis, *A Grief Observed*

These fears dominated my thoughts. Every time I used the bathroom, I checked for spotting. Before every doctor's appointment, the anticipation made me feel like I was going to be sick, always expecting to hear the worst. I had to find ways to cope with the fear and the thoughts of impending doom that seem to overshadow me. I decided to find some truths to repeat and cling to in order to combat the lies that Satan was feeding me in those moments.

I started by choosing some Bible verses and repeating them. But sometimes I was too overwhelmed by trepidation to even form the words. Instead, I found a song and put it on my phone. Every time the fear took over and thoughts of worst case scenarios began to play out in my head, I would grab my phone and play the song. I chose "Be Still, My Soul" by Ginny Owens[1]. I must have listened to this song hundreds of times in the months that followed. Here are the beautiful lyrics:

> Be still, my soul,
> The Lord is on your side.
> Bear patiently, the cross of grief or pain.
> Leave to your God, to order and provide.
> In every change He faithful will remain.
>
> Be still, my soul,
> Your best your heavenly friend,
> Through thorny waves leads to a joyful end.
>
> Be still, my soul,
> Your God will undertake
> To guide the future as He has the past.
> Your hope, your confidence let nothing shake.
> All now mysterious shall be bright at last.
>
> Be still, my soul,
> The waves and winds still know
> His voice who ruled them while He lived below.
> Be still, my soul,
> Be still, my soul, Be still.

    This song expressed all of my mixed emotions perfectly. It was a song of surrender, a song that reminded me that even though the worst case scenario

---
[1] Ginny Owens. Booklet. Something More, "Be Still, My Soul." March 2002.

in my mind was a very real possibility, God would be faithful in it. I had to learn to trust. I had to carry my baby with open hands. I had to be willing to receive and give back. I had to let go.

And in the letting go, I found peace. Why? Because when we hold on to something, we consider ourselves to be in control of it, and we aren't capable of handling that amount of responsibility. Only God gives life, and only He controls it. We have to surrender it to Him.

The other thing I did to combat the fear was to get a doppler. Every time I began to wonder if my baby's heart was still beating, all I had to do was press it to my stomach. I would rest assured when I heard the sound of a little train chugging away in my belly. I also made it a point to check for the heartbeat before every doctor's appointment. I did not want to receive any unexpected news in the office again.

At my twelve-week appointment, I went in for a regular check-up. At this point, women are considered to be in the "safe-zone" because relatively few miscarriages happen past the first trimester. Even being in the safe-zone, I felt far from safe. Nathan had an important meeting at work so he wasn't able to come to the appointment with me. The doctor asked all of the usual questions and then pulled out the doppler to listen to the heartbeat.

He moved it all around and finally said, "I'm not getting a heartbeat with the doppler. Let's take a quick look with the ultrasound."

I felt like all of the air had been sucked out of the room. The horrible familiarity of that moment was suffocating. I immediately started praying, fighting to stay calm. I had surrendered this baby to God. I had decided to trust Him no matter what, which included this. Right?

While I changed into a gown and waited in that despised ultrasound room, I grabbed my phone with shaking hands and played the song, willing myself not to cry. The doctor came in, did the ultrasound, and immediately found the heartbeat, strong and perfect. I left the appointment and walked to my car on shaking legs, still threatening to collapse.

When I got to the car, I completely broke down. I cried hysterically, sitting in the parking garage and called Nathan on the phone. Poor guy.

He answered by asking, "How was the appointment?"

When I could only respond with incomprehensible blubbering through heaving sobs, he immediately feared the worst. Eventually, I was able to calm down enough to tell him that everything was fine. I cried all the way home. Even after I got to the house, I kept crying. They were tears of relief that everything was fine, anxiety that I had faced the possibility of my greatest fear, and grief in an unexpected resurgence of emotion from our previous loss. Maybe there will always be a piece of my heart that is broken.

I would love to say that every time fear crept in, I listened to the song, surrendered, experienced peace, and moved on. That wasn't the case. Surrendering was moment by moment, hour by hour, day by day, for the entire pregnancy. Even the day that we went into the hospital to give birth, I still had a voice in the back of my mind telling me that we wouldn't be coming home with a baby. I couldn't ignore the possibility of losing another child.

When Experiencing FEAR

The enemy uses lies to create fear in our lives. Fear can be absolutely paralyzing. The best way to combat that fear is to keep God's truth close by and return to it constantly. Use the space provided at the end of this chapter to write down some Bible verses or song lyrics that you can meditate on when you are overwhelmed by fear and Satan is throwing all he has at you.

When we give in to fear, we allow Satan to steal our joy, and that is his entire goal—to steal, kill, and destroy (John 10:10). God, on the other hand, has a different plan in mind for us—to give us life and life abundantly! When we allow fear to rein in our hearts and minds, we are willingly casting away the abundant life of freedom and peace that He has for us!

Truth to Combat Fear

Truth to Combat Fear

Truth to Combat Fear

Truth to Combat Fear

NINE

REDEMPTION

"Now may the God of peace, who through the blood of the eternal covenant brought back from the dead our Lord Jesus, that great Shepherd of the sheep, equip you with every good thing for doing His will, and may He work in us what is pleasing to Him, through Jesus Christ, to whom be glory forever and ever. Amen."

Hebrews 13:20-21 NIV

I love how Jesus' teachings in the Bible turn everything about the way we think life should work completely upside down. If you want to be first, be last (Matt. 20:16). If you want to receive, give (Prov. 11:24). Those who are broken and mourn will be blessed (Matt. 5:4). If you want to truly live, you must die (Matt. 10:39).

These teachings sound crazy, but when put into practice, they prove to be true every time. These seeming paradoxes work because God sees the world from a completely different viewpoint than we do. What makes no sense in our limited framework of existence, makes perfect sense in His eternal perspective.

That is why our pain and loss, as difficult as they are, are the perfect places for God's redemption to flourish, though it seems inconceivable in the moment. There can be no redemption where there is nothing to redeem. There can be no healing unless there is first sickness. There can be no restoration where there was not first brokenness. While God did not intend for sin and death to be a part of our stories, He sure knows how to conquer them!

God has been actively redeeming what was lost from the moment Eve took a bite of the forbidden fruit.

Did you know?

The Holy of Holies was where the high priest would offer sacrifices of atonement for the sins of the people of Israel. The hem of the robe worn by the high priest was embroidered with pomegranates.

He gave the Ten Commandments in the Old Testament, created the sacrificial system, and spoke through prophets. While these methods could temporarily cover sin, they did not remove it. The Old Testament covenant was never meant to be permanent. It was a system that was impossible to adhere to, broken and hopeless as a means to redeem.

As in every story, there was a turning point: a point at which all odds seem bent towards destruction. But that is not the end. Jesus is our turning point. The Bible redeems the fall of Adam and Eve by sending a 'new Adam.' In the same way that all sin entered through one person, it is all conquered by one person, Christ on the cross (Rom. 5:12-15). Even after we chose sin, God loved us so much that He did not leave us to die in our sins (1 John 1:9).

In order to ultimately shatter the distance between us and Him, He sent His Son, His own beloved child, to die the death that we deserved. Jesus rose to life again and tore the curtain separating us from the Father. God made a way for us to be redeemed and restored to Him. Jesus' death and resurrection overthrew and continues to overthrow the former power of sin and death. Eve's curse is broken, and death now has no hold on us.

There is a new theme in scripture:

- He refreshes our soul (Ps. 23:3).
- He is seeking and saving the lost (Lk. 19:10).
- He is in the act of reconciling all things to Himself (Col. 1:20).

This restorative, reconciliatory work will not be complete until we are united with Him in eternity. And when we get there, all that was lost will be redeemed. This is one promise that we find over and over again in Scripture.

"Look at the nations and watch—and be utterly amazed. For I am going to do something in your days that you would not believe, even if you were told."
Habakkuk 1:5 (NIV)

"Forget the former things; do not dwell on the past. See, I am doing a new thing! Now it springs up; do you not perceive it? I am making a way in the wilderness and streams in the wasteland."
Isaiah 43:18-19 (NIV)

"See, I will create new heavens and a new earth. The former things will not be remembered, nor will they come to mind."
Isaiah 65:17 (NIV)

"He who was seated on the throne said, 'I am making everything new!' Then He said, 'Write this down, for these words are trustworthy and true.'"
Revelation 21:5 (NIV)

Even though this redemption is only complete in heaven, we get to see the beginnings of this reconciliation taking place on earth through the demonstration of God's grace. Wounds are healed, lives are saved, hearts are purified, and tears turn to laughter. Women do experience the joy of conceiving and giving birth. Every time that happens, it is an extension of God's grace to us, an undeserving people. You see, I had held the wrong perspective all along—it is not God who keeps us from having children, it is God who gives us the opportunity to begin with.

> This is where our promises from God come in!
> - Nothing can separate us from God's love in Christ (Rom. 8:38-39).
> - He will never leave or forsake us. (Deut. 31:6).
> - He has a plan to give us a hope and a future (Jer. 29:11).
> - He will give us peace through the journey (Phil. 4:7).

He is calling us to Himself, revealing His love in all of creation, beckoning us to lay down all of our fear, pain, doubt, idols, plans, hopes, dreams, and desires so that He can write His story of redemption on our hearts. Do you not know that He has far greater things planned for you than you could ever plan for yourself? He is making all things new!

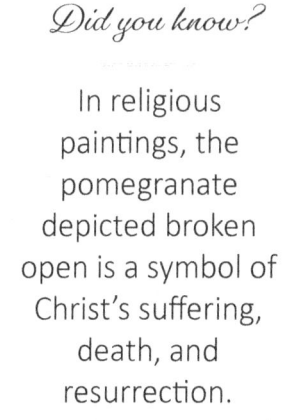

Did you know?

In religious paintings, the pomegranate depicted broken open is a symbol of Christ's suffering, death, and resurrection.

I know what you may be thinking, because I have fallen into the same trap of comparison. It is difficult not to reply by saying, 'You can say that you have been redeemed because you now have closure and a happy ending. Good for you. But I don't know if that will be the end of my story.' You are right, and I can guarantee that my story will not be your story, because God does not write the same story twice.

Let me say something very clearly, and it is my fervent prayer that you hear these words from me and accept them: God can redeem the loss that you have experienced even if you never hold a child of your own, because redemption isn't tied to any one person, thing, or experience. It is tied to Him. He is the one who redeems, through His own character, presence, and incredible love.

When He redeems, nothing exterior is needed to complete His work. He is the completion. Not only is He the Redeemer, He is the redemption. In the same way that I questioned in my journey whether I truly believed that Jesus was enough, you must also face that question for yourself in order to experience His redemption in your own life.

The Bible teaches that He who has sinned much can be forgiven much (Luke 7:47). In the same way, the depth to which we have experienced loss is the height to which we can witness God's redemption.

To illustrate this, I want to share a story from Matthew 19:16-26 (NIV). I am going to be interjecting my own commentary throughout the verses, indicated by italics.

"Just then a man came up to Jesus and asked, 'Teacher, what good thing must I do to get eternal life?'"

In other words, how can I experience redemption?

"'Why do you ask me about what is good?' Jesus replied. 'There is only One who is good. If you want to enter life, keep the commandments.'

> *Jesus, please say it louder for the people in the back, "There is only One who is good." It is common to question God's goodness in times of despair. However, Jesus teaches that not only does God qualify as good, but He is the definition of good.*

"'Which ones?' he inquired.
Jesus replied, '"You shall not murder, you shall not commit adultery, you shall not steal, you shall not give false testimony, honor your father and mother," and "love your neighbor as yourself."'
'All these I have kept,' the young man said. 'What do I still lack?'
Jesus answered, 'If you want to be perfect, go, sell your possessions and give to the poor, and you will have treasure in heaven. Then come, follow me.'"

> *Surrender it all—all of your desires, all of your plans, fears, doubts, reservations, even that little bit of entitlement to the happiness you envision for yourself. Lay it all down, and follow Jesus. We*

are afraid to do this because, just like the young man, we have a false belief that God doesn't want us to be happy. We think that by following in surrender, we must somehow learn to live being miserable and unfulfilled.

"When the young man heard this, he went away sad, because he had great wealth."

> He chose to keep the life that he had created for himself over submission, and it did not bring him fulfillment. Instead, he left sad.

"Then Jesus said to His disciples, 'Truly I tell you, it is hard for someone who is rich to enter the kingdom of heaven. Again I tell you, it is easier for a camel to go through the eye of a needle than for someone who is rich to enter the kingdom of God.'"

> The one who has never lost seems to hold on to what they have even tighter, because they have yet to learn the beauty of redemption waiting on the other side of letting go.

"When the disciples heard this, they were greatly astonished and asked, 'Who then can be saved?'"

> In other words, if this man had everything and couldn't find redemption, then who can be redeemed?

REDEMPTION

"Jesus looked at them and said, 'With man this is impossible, but with God all things are possible.'"

    Having it all is not having redemption. Having it all, but refusing to lay it down, is the greatest crisis of faith. Surrender is the way to freedom, and in that freedom, God is able to write His story of redemption in our lives.

    So hear this from me again; redemption is not tied to the circumstances of your story. It is tied to your relationship with the author of that story. God is not testing you. He does not want you to be unhappy. He wants a beautiful, whole, fulfilled, and redeemed life in which you are completely aligned with His will, so that He can effectively lead you into the fullness of His love.

    He has such amazing plans for you, just as He had for the rich young man in Matthew. What a pity that we never read another story about this man, about the things he did for God's kingdom, or his incredible faith and the relationship he shared with Jesus. He stood in front of God incarnate abiding with us and walked away. We never hear from him again. He sadly retreats to his wealth and into obscurity.

    We have the same choice in front of us, and I am praying wholeheartedly for you as you make your decision. As for me, I don't want to be that rich young man. I want to be redeemed. I want to be in the story God is writing. I want to slowly uncurl my fingers from the desires I have for myself, and open my hands filled with all the broken pieces. I want to place those pieces at the feet of Jesus and stand in awe of what He creates with them. I want to be surprised by the depth of His redemption, by the ways that He is working things together for good, whether small and intimate, or vast and inconceivable. But most of all, I want Him. More than anything else, I choose Him, and as a result of that relationship, I trust Him to make all things new in my life.

    And let me tell you, friends. He has.
    He has redeemed me in so many ways! I am going to share some of these ways with you, but only if you promise not to value the results of redemption over the Redeemer Himself. As I make this list of how God has restored so many broken things in my life, do not compare your story to mine, because God has a unique ending for you. Know that the only reason I find redemption in these moments is because of who God is. And He is the same God for you as He is for me.
    With that, I will tell you the end of the story. I will share with you the goodness of our God and how He is making all things new.

    ❧ My first daughter, Maya Grace, was born in 2016. She was ten days late, and the wait was almost unbearable. But she arrived right when she was supposed to. She was born on my thirtieth birthday. Do you remember my previous two birthdays? One was filled with hope and joy as we announced our first pregnancy to family and friends.
    The following year was filled with grief, a reminder of the loss we had experienced and the emptiness that still continued. I couldn't even bring myself to celebrate

it. And on this birthday, I received the incredible gift of holding my healthy baby in my arms. Now, every year, I get to celebrate my birthday by thanking God for His overwhelming faithfulness to me. He has redeemed this day.

🌿 Remember the local pregnancy center that I called in my distress needing someone to talk to? Remember how I started financially supporting their ministry? Well, they send out an annual newsletter with statistics about how their ministry is serving the community in different ways. It also includes some personal stories from women that they have served.

One newsletter that I received featured the story of a woman who had been considering abortion, but had decided to keep her baby as a result of the pregnancy center's encouragement and support. Her baby had been born on April nineteenth, which was the same day that Maya had been born. It was as if God were illuminating the fact that He is weaving the stories of seemingly unconnected lives into a beautiful tapestry of redemption. I was overwhelmed by the thought that my loss, through a divinely orchestrated chain of events, could have somehow contributed to the life of another baby being saved. God is using my pain to bring about redemption in the lives of others.

🌿 Do you remember the former co-worker who had asked when I would be starting a family? Standing at the copier that day in the church office, I could hardly respond because the grief was so fresh. After Maya was born, I was once again working on a project at church. I was standing at the same copier, busily printing the activity pages needed. Maya, only six months old at the time, was at my side, in her carseat in the stroller. She was peering up at me with her beautiful eyes and waving her chunky hands in the air as I worked.

Who should walk in to the office at that exact moment? It was none other than the same former co-worker who had stopped to chat with me years before. She bent over Maya and went on and on about how beautiful she was, and I smiled with pride. I was struck by the recurrence of the scene. What an amazing transformation had taken place in my life from that first encounter to the second one. Where there was once anger and offense, there is now grace and understanding. God has redeemed my relationships.

The crib that we bought on Craigslist, which sat empty in a silent nursery for nine months, was a constant place of surrender for me. I finally took it down with tears of submission, accepting that God may not have a baby in our future. Now it sits in my daughter's room, converted to a toddler bed. I sing a song to Maya every night as she goes to sleep in it. The song isn't the typical lullaby for children, but it is the same song of surrender that I listened to in all of my moments of doubt and fear throughout my pregnancy with her. It is "Be Still, My Soul" by Ginny Owens. I sing the words over her every night, many times with her sweet voice chiming in,

Be still, my soul
The Lord is on your side
Bear patiently
The cross of grief or pain

Leave to your God
To order and provide
In every season
As He has the past

Be still, my soul
The wind and waves still know
The voice who ruled them while He lived below[1]

    I give Maya back to God every night as I lay her down to sleep, knowing that even though she is with me now, there are no guarantees for tomorrow. And yet, God is love, and He is faithful. As I continually surrender, He redeems.

    In 2018 we scheduled baby bump pictures at a local park for the birth of my second daughter, Everly Joy. Maya was almost two years old at the time, and she was in rare form that day. She was running away, refusing to sit still for a picture, throwing tantrums, and making as big of a scene as possible for the photographer. I grabbed a bag of animal crackers from the car to quite literally use as bait to coax her into a few of the shots. The photo session ended prematurely when Maya dumped the whole bag of animal crackers

---

[1] Ginny Owens. Booklet. Something More, "Be Still, My Soul." March 2002.

into the fountain, and I decided that we should call it a day.

I sat on the edge of the fountain, trying to fish out the animal cracker bag, with Maya still laughing in pride at her accomplishment. I tried not to give her the satisfaction of seeing me laugh at the absurdity of the situation as animal crackers sprayed up into the air in the spout of water. Suddenly, I realized that I had sat in this very spot three years before. Do you remember the fountain? The one where I sat, all alone, shattered in pieces, at the walk to commemorate lost babies?

I was sitting in the same place, but as a completely different person. I had been broken, lost, lonely, and hopeless that day. Here I sat again, one hand on my bulging belly, embracing the child still to come, the other hand fishing out an animal cracker bag (I can't think of a better representation of the daily life of a toddler mom). I had to laugh with joy, not simply because God had blessed me so much, but more because He is who He says He is. And He loves me. The arms I so desperately needed to wrap around me that day have been there all along. He has redeemed this place.

The ultrasound room where I received the news that there was no heartbeat is the same room where I later witnessed the heartbeat of my next two babies. The machine that printed out the ultrasound picture of my lifeless child, that I had cried so many tears over, is the same machine that printed out the pictures of Maya's and Everly's perfect fingers and toes, with eyes like their daddy and cheeks like their mom.

And those fish swimming in the tank of the lobby, that haunted me for so many doctor visits with disappointing news, have witnessed many more visits with checkups for the healthy babies growing inside of me. Walking down the hall to this doctor's office used to fill me with such dread and fear that I would have a physical and emotional reaction. Now, it is a place where I have seen new life begin. God has redeemed my fear.

Mother's Day. What a day filled with mixed emotions for me! On my first Mother's Day, I carried my beloved child with no heartbeat. That day I wanted so badly to be recognized as a mother and simultaneously feared that I would crumble under the grief of that acknowledgment. On the following Mother's Day, I received the news that I was infertile. That was the day that I first started the process of coming to terms with the idea that I may never be able to have children of my own and accepting that God still had a good plan for me even in those circumstances.

The next Mother's Day, I was holding my three-week-old baby girl in my arms! Two years after that on Mother's Day, we dedicated our second daughter to God in a beautiful ceremony at our church. As I stood on the stage next to my husband and toddler, holding yet another of God's inconceivable blessings to me, I couldn't help but be awed in gratitude. Mother's Day was a day that I truly believed would always be filled with heartache, but God has filled it with unfathomable joy! He has redeemed motherhood.

✂ Remember the circular saw that was stolen from our garage the day of the ultrasound? We didn't miss it for a long time after that, with no spark of motivation to create anything. Eventually, though, we bought a new saw, and we used it to cut the wood to build our kitchen table. Every day, I sit at this table and share meals with the family I never imagined would be a part of my story. I reach across the wooden surface that my husband and I sanded and stained together to grasp the tiny hands next to mine. Over it we offer thanks to the God who has walked with us through every step of this journey. He is making all things new.

✂ The painting that Nathan and I created to announce the conception of our first child hangs in the living room of our home. It started out as a creation of joy and expectation. It turned into a tangible memory of our lost little one. Now it is a constant reminder of God's faithfulness. He has redeemed this memory.

✂ Finally, there is my child that I lost. I do not know if my sweet baby was a boy or girl, but God does, because He created him or her in His own image. He lovingly knit my child together in my womb. And because of the price that Jesus paid on the cross, my child is currently in the presence of God in heaven, experiencing eternal life more fully than we can fathom here on earth. By His incredible grace, God has redeemed my baby.

REDEMPTION

In the depths of depression I had wondered if I would ever experience joy again. If I would ever laugh at something funny, if I would ever have a lighthearted skip in my step for no apparent reason, if I would ever feel the sun on my face and experience that peaceful stillness in my soul. I thought that I would never be completely healed, that I would always harbor a sensitive, wounded place in my heart, and that my old self was forever lost.

It is true that I will never be the same, and my old self is gone, but it has been replaced by a person who understands the depths of peace, joy, and gratitude more fully than I thought possible. I have a greater appreciation for who God is, and what He is doing in my life, because I have walked with Him through the valleys as well as the mountaintops. He has restored my joy. He has filled me with His peace. He is making me new.

> "Jesus Christ did not come into this world to make bad people good; He came into this world to make dead people live."
> - Lee Strobel

I could go on for a lot longer with my list of how God has brought redemption to my life. John puts it best, "Jesus did many other things as well. If every one of them were written down, I suppose that even the whole world would not have room for the books that would be written" (John 21:25 NIV).

And I know that even as I write, God is still continuing the process of redemption in my life, and it will not be fully complete until I reunite with Him in His glorious presence. There is still so much more to come!

As I look back over these moments of redemption, I am struck by the reality that God is outside of time. We see and experience life linearly, and we are concentrated on the moment, with no way to see what is to come. But when God sees our life, He sees all of it at once. He knows what is to come, and He sees it as a part of so many other peoples' stories that we will never know about. He is orchestrating every individual story across languages, continents, and millennia into one vast redemptive symphony declaring His majesty.

Why do we still doubt His ability to redeem? As I pray, He sees the fulfillment of that prayer already accomplished. As I experience loss, He sees the redemption of that loss already complete. As I question, He sees the answers written into my future. And that is why I can trust Him with today and with the future, whatever it may bring. Because He is today, tomorrow, and forever.

⊰ When Experiencing REDEMPTION ⊱

There is a place at the end of this chapter for you to write down ways in which you see God's redemption demonstrated in your life. This is definitely a practice that you can continue for years as God progressively reveals new areas of your life that He is making new.

I am writing this book years after my miscarriage. My journey to redemption has been slow, painful, and accented by seasons of backsliding. There have been many attempts on my part to retake control of my story. Don't expect to be ready to surrender it all and find redemption simply because you have finished reading the final chapter of this book. Remember that God is outside of time, and trust that He knows best when to write in each part of your story. Redemption is a process that continues until we reach heaven, and we finally know Him fully, even as we are fully known (1 Cor. 13:12).

God's Redemption

God's Redemption

God's Redemption

God's Redemption

EPILOGUE

> *Did you know?*
>
> Solomon uses the image of a pomegranate to describe the temples of his beloved (Song of Sol. 4:3).

After I finished writing this manuscript, I formed a group of women who had experienced miscarriage, to read through the book and offer their insight. The night before I gave them their copies, I prayed over each manuscript and each woman who would read it. I knew that it would take courage for them to read through the book, re-live their pain in its pages, persevere through the work of grieving from loss, and seek God's redemption in their individual stories. As I was praying for them, I thanked God for using me to be a part of His redemption story and for showing me His unchanging character through every season of my life. And then I found myself thanking Him for my loss. Right after the words left my mouth, I stopped in realization that this was the first time that I had ever thanked Him for my loss. And, even more amazingly, I genuinely meant it.

I can't believe that the one thing I swore that I would never do while listening to my pastor speak on trials all of those years ago, was exactly what was happening. I can genuinely thank God for the loss that I experienced, because it allowed me to see Him, to know

Him, to trust Him, and to love Him in ways that I never would have otherwise.

    My next thought was how sad it was that it had taken me five years to reach the point of true gratitude. Five years! Redemption does not take place overnight. And yet, how could it have taken me so long, especially when He has done such incredible things in my life? I have thanked Him for everything else, yes—the redemption, the blessings, His character that He demonstrated throughout the process. However, not until that moment, after writing everything down in one place and giving God the credit He deserved for His wondrous works in my life, did I finally express gratitude for the loss that set the entire redemption promise into motion. Didn't I tell you at the beginning that this book was not about me becoming a mother, but rather about me becoming a child? I am fully embracing my role as God's child.

    In the same way that I prayed for the first group of women to read this book, I pray for you, dear friend.

    I pray that God's presence would be so tangible in your grief that you feel His arms around you.

    I pray that God's grace would pour over you as you navigate emotional instability and lose confidence in your self-sufficiency.

    I pray that God's truth would be engraved on your heart and mind as you explore the spiritual questions you face, and that His Word would be living and active.

I pray that His faithfulness would overwhelm you to the point of utter amazement and bring you to tears in awe and worship.

I pray that God's sovereignty would drive out all fear, and that you would find Him trustworthy in your darkest hours.

I pray that His redemption would flood your life in amazing ways that are intimate and personal, that allow you to hear Him whispering to your broken heart, "I am making all things new!"

I pray that the story God continues to write in your life would be so beautiful and bring Him so much glory that you can't wait to share it with others.

I pray that His restoration in you will be so complete that you will one day be able to thank Him for your loss.

I know that my expectations for God's work in your life are high. Right now you may be thinking that it is impossible. I once thought the same. But I can assure you that it is more than possible. Even my boldest prayers for you cannot begin to challenge the plans that He has in store! The depth of God's redemption truly is inconceivable.

Shout for joy, you heavens;
rejoice, you earth;
burst into song, you mountains!
For the Lord comforts His people
and will have compassion on His afflicted ones.
But Zion said, "The Lord has forsaken me,
the Lord has forgotten me."
Can a mother forget the baby at her breast,
and have no compassion on the child she has borne?
Though she may forget,
I will not forget you!
See, I have engraved you on the palms of my hands;
Then you will know that I am the Lord;
those who hope in me will not be disappointed.
Then all mankind will know that I, the Lord,
am your Savior, your Redeemer,
the Mighty One of Jacob.

Isaiah 49:13-16a, 23b, 26b (NIV)

A LETTER FROM GOD

My Dear Child,

My heart is breaking with yours right now. I have not forgotten you, but I am right here beside you, present in your pain. You are so precious to me, and I bottle up each of your tears as you grieve the loss of your child. This tragedy was not my plan—it is the result of the sin of a fallen world, far from the perfect place I had originally created for you, dear child. I love you so much, and I am devastated that you have to experience such pain.

I understand your pain all too well. I also experienced the loss of a child when I sent my own Son to earth to die an excruciating death and be separated from me. But I have redeemed that loss, because the result is that your child is experiencing eternal life with me in Heaven at this very moment. I am eagerly looking forward to the day when the pain of this world will be redeemed in the same way, for your present suffering will end and every tear will be wiped away in the glory of Heaven!

Satan wants to use this loss for his own purposes: to steal your joy, kill your faith, and destroy your future. But I am with you, and I am greater than he is. If you continue to trust me through this dark time, our relationship will grow so much stronger than it was before. I will use this new strength to prepare you for other challenges and victories in the days ahead that can only be overcome with faith that has faced doubt.

    I know that you have a lot of questions right now, and asking them is good. Look in my Word and I will show you the answers. Listen to the truth that you find there, rather than the lies that the evil one is whispering in your ear. If you can continue to put your faith in me, then even this terrible loss will result in something beautiful and good. Do not give Satan the satisfaction of winning the battle for your heart and mind!

    I know that you have certain plans in mind and are worried about the timing in which those plans will be complete, but my timing is perfect. I command the sun to rise and set, and I alone know what tomorrow holds. I am going to ask you to trust me, and rest in the knowledge that I have your best interests in mind. I have a good and perfect plan for you. I know each of your children intimately, for I have created them. I know them by name and love them even more than you do! I have a plan not only for your future, but also for today! You are right where you are for a reason, and even the waiting has a purpose.

    I know that you feel betrayed by your own body, and you feel like you are unable to do what you were created to do. Your body is not broken—you are fearfully and wonderfully made in my own image! I have created you and know every detail, from the hairs on your head to the number of days of your life. I know each part that is working properly, as well as those that are working against you. This body, which seems to have betrayed you, is only temporary and will one day be made new, yet it is still my very own creation! In the ways that it has failed you, I will one day restore.

I know that you are hurting. I know that it is difficult to think about anything other than what you have lost. Just remember that there are many things to be grateful for even in the pain. Hold tightly to those who love you and the blessings that you have as you work through the grieving process. A grateful heart that counts its blessings is one that can withstand even the most devastating of losses.

I know that you feel like this is the end. You had so much to look forward to, and now you aren't sure how to move forward into the emptiness. Your heart is so shattered that you wonder if it will ever be whole again, if it will ever experience joy again. Let me assure you—this is far from the end! My plan for you is not yet complete. You can rest knowing that I, your Father, who love you more than you can imagine, hold your future in my hands.

I am orchestrating the work of redemption, and I am making all things new! I have so much more in store for you. Bring me the broken pieces of your heart, your hopes, your dreams, your desires, and your fears. Entrust them to me. Take my hand, dear child. Lay your head on my chest, release your pain and your fears and your hurt, and rest. Let me show you what I will do...

I love you more than you can imagine,
God

ABOUT THE AUTHOR

Erin Greneaux is a wife and mom to two daughters, Maya and Everly, in Lafayette, Louisiana. A graduate of Baylor University, Erin has worked in Christian ministry for over a decade in children's ministry, missions, education in at-risk communities, and curriculum development. Erin is an accomplished writer, with published works in poetry, short story, magazine articles, musicals, a young adult novel, Spy Recruit, and a Christian devotional, Learnable Moments for Moms.

Erin is passionate about helping women learn to grow in their relationship with Christ and serve Him with their talents in each unique season of life. She enjoys ministering to Christian moms through her blog, www.greneauxgardens.com while focusing on raising her girls at home.

Also by Erin Greneaux:
Learnable Moments for Moms:
100 Devotions to Discover God in the Everyday

Meet my daughters, Maya and Everly. Maya is a headstrong two year old, leaping into each day with enthusiasm and her fair share of strong-willed tantrums. Her baby sister, Everly, is all smiles, giggles, and pure joy! For 100 days, we will step into Maya's shoes (if we can find them!) and see what we can learn as moms about God's relationship with us, His will for our lives, and how we can continue to grow into children who follow Him.

As moms we are constantly on the lookout for teachable moments with our kids, but this book will help us identify the many learnable moments that God places in our lives every day. The world around us, complete with the chaos of raising kids, is the very classroom that God wants to use to connect us to Him. It may be a feat to get out of the house without something sticky on our clothes, but that doesn't mean we can't have a growing, challenging, and life-giving personal relationship with God.

Each day includes:
- Relatable Story from Motherhood
- Biblical Scripture
- Practical Application
- Prayer Prompt
- Question for Reflection

PICTURES

Left: The picture that I took on my birthday at the bed and breakfast from the hammock. Innocent bliss!

Below: The painting Nathan and I made to announce our pregnancy, which hangs in our living room.

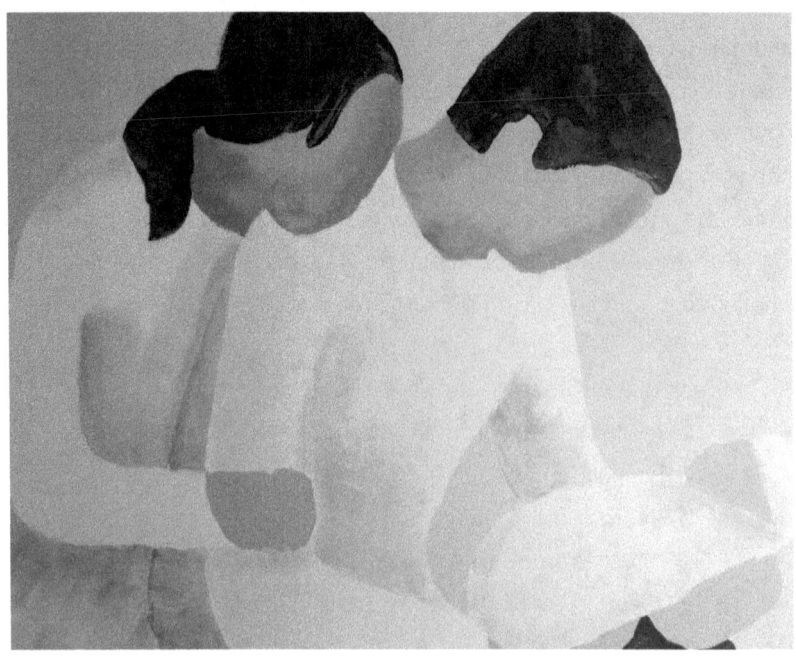

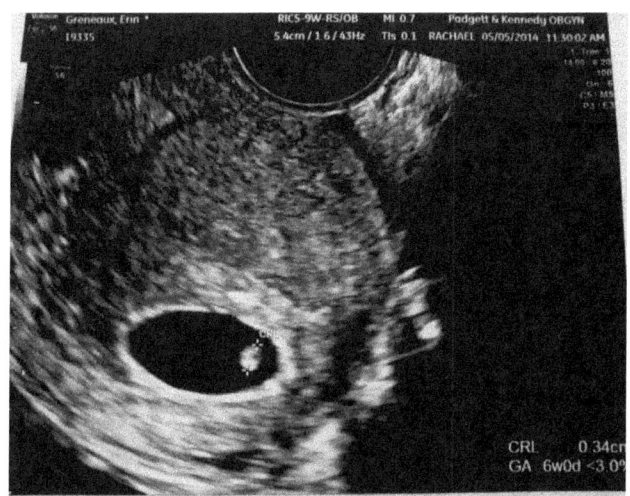

Left: The ultrasound photo from our first baby.

Right: The crib that sat in the empty nursery for nine months.

Below: The garden where I experienced God's gentle healing and direction.

Left: Releasing the balloon at the walk to commemorate my baby at the pregnancy loss event.

Right: Nathan and I at the Summer Palace in China.

Below: Nathan and I at the Cliffs of Moher in Ireland.

Above: The infamous baby bump pictures, complete with the animal crackers (before they ended up in the fountain).

Below: Our family!

www.ingramcontent.com/pod-product-compliance
Lightning Source LLC
Chambersburg PA
CBHW071202070526
44584CB00019B/2888